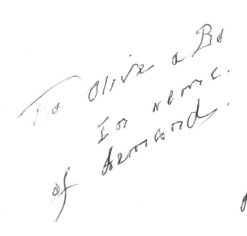

Born Minus

From Shoeshine Boy to News Publisher
An Italian-American Journey

Born Minus

From Shoeshine Boy to News Publisher
An Italian-American Journey

Armand Miele

The Citizens' Publishing
Corporation of Rockland
Nanuet, NY

Copyright 2011 Armand Miele

ISBN 978-1-257-94170-4

Dedication

To my wife, Ofelia Esguerra Miele, M.D. She gave me a chance by believing in me, and by letting me believe in her. If I didn't have my wife, I'd have been gone a long time ago. She saved me many times, literally. I owe her my life.

We've been married for over 40 years and are still in love, even though she was and still is too good for me. She married me, a construction worker, and I hope that she still believes she wasn't crazy to do it. We made it work together. Without her, there's no way we would have what we do today.

This book will tell it all.

St. John the Baptist Church, Yonkers, NY, May 10, 1967

Contents

Introduction

My father began writing "Born Minus" about 10 years ago, early in his 70s. Before that, his life stories and political opinions had existed only as long conversations around the dinner table, over a glass or two of wine; or as heated discussions with his friends, colleagues, and later, political acquaintances. I know that even at this point in his life, well into his 80s, my father is not done arguing or telling stories, nor will he be content to simply hand this book to people, whether they agree with him or not. Instead, he will keep talking, prefacing every story and argument with a withering look, and saying, "Haven't you read my book?" So, reader, consider yourself one of the lucky ones who will be able to say, "Why, of course!"

Whether you avidly follow current events, enjoy new perspectives on history, or just appreciate a great story and good old common sense, there is something here for you.

You can read Part One, "Born Minus", from beginning to end, as a story, since the chapters are arranged chronologically; but each chapter can also be read on its own. While the author has been as accurate as possible, keep in mind that the first part of this book is based mostly on his memories, and the memories of those close to him. In certain parts of the memoir, where a name was forgotten, the editors have invented names, for ease of reading. Events, however, have not been invented. The author hopes that you will accept the stories in the spirit that they were first told to family and friends, as parables for life's lessons, based on his personal experiences.

Part Two of this book, "Miele's Musings," collects a portion of the author's writings for the Rockland County Times. The chapters of Part Two, also, can either be read in order, with each central theme building on the last, or separately, allowing the reader to focus on a particular set of ideas. The author has given the most recent publication dates, but many of these Musings have been reprinted several times, in varying forms, since 1998. They represent a lifetime of American experience and thought.

I join my father in hoping that you enjoy this book. It was a labor of love, not only for his family, but for all of you readers, who he feels privileged to address.

Donna Lee Miele
July 5, 2011

Foreword

By Dylan Skriloff

The story of Armand Miele is the story of America—one man's fascinating journey through the landscape of the real American dream.

Some may believe the term American dream is a cliché, but it's more than that—it's a truth.

For Armand Miele, that truth means every American must be determined to fight and win, to make his or her own path in living life, and ultimately to enjoy success.

If that isn't a value we can all agree on, I don't know what is. Though Miele grew up in the Depression-era Bronx, where people had to struggle just to put food on the table and shoes on their feet, today's society should value the same determination to survive and succeed.

In fact, I'm convinced that if more Americans would adjust their attitudes to the old-fashioned and hard working one that Armand Miele preaches, many of our problems would be put behind us in an instant.

I've certainly come closer to achieving those hard-working ideals since I've met Armand Miele, who was my direct boss for about a year and a half at the Rockland County Times. Miele is currently publisher emeritus of the newspaper, which he rescued from bankruptcy in the mid-1990s and which has been in existence since 1888. He took this role after a long and illustrious career in real estate, and a taste of politics, to assist in his efforts to reform Rockland County.

As editor-in-chief of this paper, I have been put right into the mix of everything going on in Rockland, and with Miele's good counsel largely to credit, have done quite well. I couldn't have done it without learning to push forward.

I often think of a time a few years back when I was helping Miele move some of our newspaper boxes, machines that dispense newspapers for 50 cents. Though I was young and in perfect health, I would groan to myself every time I had to pick up one of the heavy machines. Due purely to mental whining, it would take me a while to move even one. Then I saw Miele, 78 years old at the time and in less than the best shape due to many health issues, pick up the same heavy machine and move it right across the street in half the time it took me. Instantly I said, "Wow, that old guy knows how to get things done. I'd better shape up."

Miele has lived through a lot of history and doesn't mind sharing what he's seen, as you will see in this book. His story will give you a taste of what life for a struggling Italian family was like in the 1930s. You will gain a window into the old Italian culture and how Miele transitioned to the American culture. You will feel the old streets of New York City. You will see, through Miele's life story, what universal values bind Americans together—and you will also hear his frustrations with those who are undermining our values!

Miele is famous in Rockland County for publishing his editorials known as "Miele's Musings," a compilation of which comprises the second half of the book. In his Musings, Miele takes a no-holds barred approach to his audience, unleashing exactly what is on his mind and how he sees things. Because he has so been so active in business and life, Miele's opinions are usually informed by his own experiences, adding an extra air of authority.

You won't always agree with Miele's Musings, but they will definitely fascinate you! You will often see conservative political thinking in action, in a way that is not portrayed in the mainstream media.

What I find most interesting about Miele is that he doesn't give up, he sees things through and is persistent. If you knew him, you'd say the same. He's a fighter, often an underdog, "born minus" as the title of the book says, but he's pulled some surprising victories from his sleeves.

In Rockland County, Miele was the driving force behind removing the illegal Spring Valley toll on I-287. The state had no jurisdiction for a toll in Rockland and with little help from local politicians, Miele was able to do the research and legwork to have the toll removed. Recently, an analyst from the County Executive's office told me he believes the removal of the toll has added as much as $1 billion to the economy of Rockland County in the last 15 years. It makes sense. Think of all the time Rocklanders have saved and all the traffic jams that have been avoided.

Miele fought to defeat school budgets he found wasteful, to build a new county courthouse in record time after years of delays and even to have smoking regulated more tightly in restaurants, so non-smokers did not have to suffer. He's run for New York state assembly, Ramapo town supervisor and Rockland county executive. He helped found the Village of Montebello, where he still lives with his wife, next door to their daughter, son-in-law, and five grandchildren. In Clarkstown, he's known as the man who built up and managed several properties on Main St. in Nanuet.

As you will read in the pages of this book, he's also battled health issues that have plagued him much of his life. Yet those health issues did not stop him from being a good father and husband. Miele was on the cutting edge for treatment of celiac disease, when in his early 40s the simple gluten sensitivity nearly cost him his life. He survived cancer at a relatively early age, and then later he struggled through diabetes, kidney failures and many other challenges, but his mind always remained focused on getting things done for his family, his business and Rockland County.

Miele has one more fight he'd like to win, and most Rocklanders would like to jump in the ring and help him out. Get the Metropolitan Transit Authorty (MTA) out of Rockland County! The MTA taxes Rockland for services it doesn't even use, basically grabbing $60 million a year in excess tax money out of the pockets of suburbanites and putting it in the pocket of Manhattan residents.   In the last three years, since the infamous MTA payroll tax was proposed and passed (the eighth tax in Rockland to pay for MTA services), the issue has become a cause célèbre...but if you look at Miele's Musings editorials you will see he has been talking about the problem for years.

Read this story of Miele's life, from his youth growing up in the Bronx straight through to his career as a successful businessman and influential figure in Rockland County politics, and you will get a taste of America and a taste of life. The book is full of amusing anecdotes about life, love and work.

Miele had no special connections with high society, did not come from a privileged family, and did not even have the resources to attend college, yet he made himself into a genuine success story through the intrinsically American characteristics of hard work and a fighter's attitude. If he can do it, so can you.

Enjoy the book, I know you will!

Dylan Skriloff
Associate Publisher and
Editor-in-Chief
Rockland County Times

Part One

Born Minus, A Memoir

ARMAND MIELE

ROCKLAND COUNTY TIMES weekly

SQUARE UNDER THE SPOTLIGHT

Above Left: My mother and my brother Augie pose for a passport picture circa 1923

Above: Gene Crescenzi and me at P.S. 74 in the Bronx, 1941

Left: My shoebox

Childhood

Gifts from the Great Depression

The Great Depression is notorious in American history for bread lines, ruined fortunes, and rampant poverty. But this isn't the whole story. For my family of Italian immigrants, escaping the devastation of World War I, America was still a land of promise. The Bronx tenement I was born in, three flights up from Hughes Avenue in December of 1928, was one of many occupied by the Italian-American families that became the backbone of the Arthur Avenue neighborhood. For us, the Great Depression was not only a time of struggle, but of holding onto a decent lifestyle through practicality, and of gratitude for the chance to start anew.

My earliest memory is going up those three flights of stairs to our apartment. Holding my mother's hand, I would climb one flight and think I was at the top, then get turned around to climb the next flight. And that wasn't even the top; we had to turn and climb one more before arriving at our doorstep. The stairs seemed endless.

When we could afford to move to a first floor apartment on 188th Street, my parents must have felt we had really arrived. That December was the first Christmas I remember having a tree. It was only a little bush on a table, but it was complete with lights, a real spectacle for boys like my brother Frank and me. I had just turned three, and Frank was only a year older. Jimmy and Augie, our older brothers, were five and six.

Christmas Eve, Frank got me out of bed to sneak a last look at the tree. "Armand," he said.

"Yeah, Frank?"

"Maybe he'll come, huh?"

"Maybe?"

"Yeah, let's wait and see!"

"Okay!"

I would do anything my older brothers asked of me, especially Frank. But I guess I couldn't stay awake, because later, back in my bed, I woke up to a loud bang from the kitchen. I heard footsteps, a whistle, and I swear, I thought I heard the reindeer talking to each other in Italian. "*'Zite!* Be quiet!" I wanted to go peek at Santa but I wasn't brave enough to leave my bed, where I slept with brothers on either side, and eventually I drifted back to sleep.

Christmas morning, I woke to the sound of shouting and, just like every morning, to the smell of my mother's strong Italian coffee. I jumped out of bed and ran to the living room.

It was Augie and Jimmy shouting, running around, and waving some muddy-looking scraps of paper that turned out to be dollar bills. Frank crept out from under the stove; he slept there when it was cold. He ran in with big eyes and pulled the papers down from the tree, handing one to me.

"It's a dollar, Armand! It's money! He came! He came!" We yelled and jumped up and down like our brothers.

My parents, at the breakfast table, told us to be quiet, "*'Zite!*", but with smiles on their faces.

And then Jimmy shouts, "Pop, I saw you put the money on the tree. I saw you. It wasn't Santa, it was you. Santa didn't come! There is no Santa."

Well, that was it. My father's smile disappeared. He said nothing. In fact in all the years after, he never brought it up. But we never received a Christmas gift from him again.

This was our first lesson in honoring the dollars that my father earned, of which my mother kept track to the penny, with the work of his back, as a day laborer and stonecutter. My brothers and I understood without being told that bringing in the daily meal was a struggle.

As we got older, we learned to never ask for the "Americano" things that other children had: milk and cookies, baseballs and bats, picture books. We learned to take care of whatever we owned. We learned to pay our own way.

I remember my father buying shoes for us only once, in the spring of 1936, when I was seven years old. Winter was supposed to be over, but the coming spring had brought only slush and mud, not a real thaw. My sneakers were almost worn out. All winter I lined them with newspaper to cover the holes in the soles, but there were so many now that I came home with my feet wet and cold as ice almost every day.

We followed Pop to the shoe store, but he kept on walking.

"Pop, wait! We passed it," one of us said. It was probably Jimmy, the only one who would ever speak up to my father.

"No," Pop said. "We got to go to the other place, to get the good shoes, with arches. Shoes for church."

"Church? What for?"

"You boys get your Communion soon. *Dopo la Pasqua*, after Easter."

For four pairs of shoes, Pop laid out four five-dollar bills. Who knows how long he had to work to make that money—with food and rent to pay for, it might have taken him months to save $20. The sweat that came down his face as he put down the money was like blood. I didn't dare ask for sneakers too. The next day, Frankie and I started saving up for pairs of two-dollar sneakers, which we bought ourselves a month later, in the shoe store closer to home. We couldn't wear the church shoes in the street every day. Our mother would have killed us.

My brothers and I made our money cleaning other people's shoes. Although our neighborhood was strictly working class, many Manhattan office workers lived nearby. They took the train down to the city every day, and they relied on the street kids for shoe-shines.

I made my first shoebox when I was seven, right after school let out. It was a little wooden box that I filled with brushes, rags, and shoe polish. It had a stand for a customer's foot on top, and a strap to carry it over my shoulder. My brothers by this time were shining shoes every day to make money for my mother's groceries, and why shouldn't I?

It was a relief to be outside, even in the street, in the summer. The tenement got hot as anything. All winter we froze in the bedrooms, because the steam heat went only to the kitchen and the living room. The winter that I turned seven, from December of 1935 to the thaw in 1936, was the coldest in 100 years. By July, though, we had to go out to the fire escape to get any rest. With four boys in the bed there was no way you could sleep. There was no breeze in the bedroom, even with the front door, the street door, and the windows wide open, all night. The tenements kept out the rain, but that's about it.

Sleeping outside, I woke at dawn. Augie, who my father relied on to get the rest of us to work, would already be at the table, dunking a hunk of stale bread into coffee. Frank might be there too, falling asleep over his cup. Ma would be feeding Catherine, the baby, a little egg from a spoon.

"Come on, baby," Ma would say in English, and then in Italian, "*Mangi'un po'*, Catarin, come on, *mangi*."

Jimmy might be standing in front of the open icebox. Ma would shout, "Close that ice box, the ice will melt!"

The icebox was my mother's single fancy, modern thing. She wasn't really worried about the ice. She shouted because there wasn't any food in the icebox. I'm the one who had to bring the milk pail to the grocer to get our milk ration, and I remember how quickly it would empty.

If I was lucky that morning, Catherine would push Ma's spoon away, and Ma would let her down from the chair. Ma would smile and wave me over. "Come on, Armand, you eat. She don't want no more."

I hurried to the table to get the leftover egg, beaten with sugar and a little sweet wine. It was delicious. There were never enough eggs to make for everyone; my mother only made one for the baby.

Ma turned on the radio and sang in broken English as she put away the cups and plates. "Be sure it's-a true, when you say I love-a you, it's a sin-a, to tell a lie..." She learned most of her English this way. Pop learned his on the job.

Pop would have left already, while it was still dark. All the stone cutting and construction jobs were in Manhattan. If he didn't get there very early, there would be a long line of workers ahead of him, and he would be turned away.

In the summer, when construction work started, we boys had to help out on the farm since my father was gone so early. Our farm was an abandoned lot where Pop raised rabbits and chickens, and grew tomatoes and all sorts of vegetables: eggplants, peppers, zucchini and other squashes. For a few years, he grew peaches, too, big and sweet, from a single tree, before the birds discouraged him. We headed to the farm before starting our regular work of shining shoes at the Arthur Avenue Market.

The four of us went out together with our shoeboxes slung over our shoulders. Augie carried the scythe, leading the rest of us to where Pop left the wheelbarrow, loaded with burlap sacks.

We walked the two miles to the farm, passing through the park and the empty lots where the grass grew long. Augie cut it, and the rest of us stuffed our sacks. As we shoved fresh grass into the rabbit cages, Jimmy kept yelling, "Damn these rabbits!"

I don't know what he had against the rabbits, except that he hated getting dirty while gathering their food. In the winter we fed them whatever vegetable scraps we found in the waste barrels near the Arthur Avenue pushcarts. You couldn't help getting a little messy, leaning over the barrels and trying to walk on slippery old vegetables and slush. Pop warned us not to feed them celery and parsley, because they would get sick, but Jimmy packed his sack with celery and parsley anyway. He didn't know that I would go in after him and take it out of the cages.

By the time we finished feeding the rabbits and got back, the market had come alive. The pushcarts were opened up. Each pushcart was actually a little wooden store on wheels, with shelves and even little cabinets for wares. At the end of the day, the pushcarts would line up along the sidewalks, shutters down and locked. During the day, the shutters were wide open, propped up with sticks, and the shelves were loaded with food. The vendors shouted to the passing shoppers, hawking their wares. *"Signora, guarda! Milone com'u'fuoco!"* Look, madam! Melon like fire! *"Mangi'o pesce e morte mai!"* Eat fish and never die! *"Yimmee-yimmee-apple!"* And of course the bean man yelling, *"Hey, fazooool!"*

Everybody sold something at the market. I started out at only four years old. My hands were too small to hold up the lemons and tomatoes like the pushcart vendors, so I sold shopping bags. I would buy them at two for three cents and sell them for two cents each, a half-cent profit on each bag. I bought a piece of chocolate cake with my first two cents profit, and then gave all the rest of my money to my mother.

Now that I was older, the other boys and I spread out along the sidewalks to shine shoes. It was five cents a shine. Slowly, over the course of the day, my pockets filled enough to jingle.

Once, a man came to me wearing old-fashioned high shoes—but I mean high!—with buttons instead of laces. He had four pennies in his hand, and he asked for a shine.

"It's a nickel a shine, mister," I told him.

He tried to chisel me. "Look, son, you don't understand. A nickel is just one coin. I've got four pennies." He held out the pennies in his hand, like I wouldn't know the difference between four and five cents. How could he expect me to shine those high shoes for four cents? I could have charged extra!

"A shine is five cents," I said, and I picked up my shoebox and walked away. I heard him cussing behind my back, in English, calling me an ungrateful WOP. I didn't let it bother me, though. There were certain people you had to keep away from in the street. Once, a burly policeman caught me, called me a dirty Guinea, and kicked my shoebox in the street. I got to keep my shoebox, because one of the guys from the neighborhood stood up for me and the cop was afraid. But lots of boys had them taken away. Then they would have to go down to the station to pick them up.

At the end of the day I was proud to have two pockets full of nickels to bring home to my mother. It didn't occur to me, when I started out shining shoes, to keep any money for myself, so I was shocked when I first saw Jimmy knot some nickels into his handkerchief, then throw it in the gutter. "Jimmy, what are you doing!"

"Ssh!" he said. "I'll come back and get it before they clean the streets tomorrow."

"What do you get with that money anyway?" Augie said to Jimmy. "Cigarettes? You don't even smoke."

"What do you care?"

I never kept money from my mother, but I learned later that throwing it in the gutter was the only way to keep it without lying to Ma. She kept our earnings in a jar over the sink for the groceries, and no amount of asking would get her to give us back a penny. That grocery money was too precious. I asked her for a nickel, once. I don't remember why I wanted it, but I wanted it bad—I wasn't above throwing a tantrum, lying down and kicking the floor. That nickel was mine! I had worked for it! But she wouldn't give it to me. The milk pail was empty, and there were mouths to feed. Even if she herself went without, which I now know she often did, she couldn't give up a nickel.

At the end of the day, when we came around the corner of our block, we could see Ma in the kitchen window, rolling and cutting the pasta dough. Later, as Pop came down the street, she would throw the pasta into the water she had simmering on the back of the stove. The pasta would be done by the time he walked into the apartment. She'd pour the tomato and meat gravy over it, and we'd eat.

Dinnertime was the only time that we saw my father during the day. He was very quiet, tired, I guess, after working hard all day. But sometimes, he mentioned memories from World War I. He was taken prisoner by the Germans, and was sick in prison for a while. My brothers and I kept still for a moment to listen.

"They use the gas," he would say, with a grimace. But he never told anything beyond that. He didn't describe "The Horrors of Gas Warfare," like they did in my scrapbook newspaper clippings. I also had pictures I found from Armistice Day, when World War I ended, and everyone in New York City celebrated in the streets. I only learned years later about the helplessness of the Italian infantry against German artillery and gas attacks in the battle of Caporetto in 1917. My father never gave us specifics; I could only wonder what exactly he had suffered. Instead, he would go on to a story from the old country that we already knew, like the one about *Zi' Angelo* selling his old donkey to the gypsies, then buying it back by mistake.

The talk at dinner was all in Italian. We didn't speak it outside the neighborhood, since the other children in school would make fun of us. But on the other hand, you didn't speak English outside of school, because then your friends called you Americano.

My parents never really got used to America. They kept the old ways. My brothers and I thought they were out of date, and would never understand the way things work here. To get his news, for instance, my father wouldn't pay the nickel to get a newspaper and read it at home, like the Americans. It wouldn't have been hard for him to find a paper on the sidewalk in the market for free, like I did, but he didn't do that either, or even listen to the radio, like my mother. Instead, every night after dinner, my father had to take his walk in the neighborhood, no matter the weather. He visited with the other old men, saying hello, having a cup of coffee or a cigarette in the rain, in the snow, in the dark. They never looked like they were saying anything important. Often they didn't even look like they were having fun. Yet that's how he got his news. That's how he learned of Roosevelt winning the election, how he heard about new jobs coming up, how he found out who was a racketeer and who was an honest man. He didn't tell us that life was like this all over Italy; it had been for hundreds of years, still is, and may still be for a hundreds of years into the future.

We didn't know it, but these men were helping each other to learn what was needed for their families to struggle and survive in this new country. These men with their broken English, holding on to the old-fashioned Italian ways, were the reason we could sleep on hot summer nights with our doors and windows wide open.

My mother wouldn't accompany my father on his walks. There was the cleaning up to do, the baby to put to bed, the diapers or other laundry to put to soak in the bathtub. Everything was done by hand. It all had to be done before Pop came home ready for bed, because the minute he walked in the door all the lights must go out. During the day, my mother went to the market with the other women, and might invite them in for a cup of coffee, always making her friends laugh. But as soon as Pop was home, he laid down the law.

My mother came from Bisaccia, a small village in Italy, in the mountains east of Naples. She arrived at Ellis Island in 1924 at the age of 19, along with my brother Augie, who was nine months old at the time. My father, who came from the even smaller village of Andretta, was there to meet her. They had married in Italy, and he had gone ahead to set up house and find work.

Who knows how my parents came to be married! The merchants lived in Bisaccia, while Andretta was a village of farmers. My father was always the one with the long, serious face. My mother said his whole family looked that way. When we would gather as a family on rainy Sunday afternoons, she pointed out their faces in the slim family album she put together, and in the blurred old photographs they really did all look the same, no smiles on thin faces. How she laughed! She was the only one who could take the serious look off Pop's face. We played cards on those afternoons, just played, no money involved. My father always had that same serious look on his face, like all the Mieles from Andretta. While he was looking at his cards, my mother and Jimmy would cheat. Pop would pretend he didn't understand why they were laughing so hard, but then he would smile and shake his head.

When my father came home for bed, he would turn off the lights before anyone else was ready. He might catch my mother while she was still in the middle of changing Catherine, and she would holler, "*Lasciala*! Leave it!"

"*Ed'u'sprech'*," he'd growl, "It's a waste."

"*Lasciala*!" she'd repeat. "When I'm dead, I'll sit in the dark!"

***

Some summer mornings, Augie and Jimmy would go out early with Pop, and I'd be on my own with Frankie. I spent most of my time him. When he was eight years old, and I was seven, we were almost the same size. When we walked together down Arthur Avenue, there was always someone who called me Frank or who called him Armand.

One of those mornings when we were on our own, on our way to the farm, we saw a moving truck stopped at a light on Pelham Parkway, the long straight road that we had to walk for two miles. Frankie blurted out, "Let's hitch a ride!"

I stared at the bent, rusty bumper that was as high as my chest. Frankie was already climbing on, telling me I had to follow. I knew my mother wouldn't like it, but we were on our own. I was the little brother, and there was no time to argue.

"It's only for a mile, or something!"

He told me to hold on to a certain spot. I was supposed to jump off when the truck stopped at the traffic light near the farm. It was okay at first, because the truck didn't go very fast and Frank was with me, laughing.

Well, of course the traffic light did not turn red. It was green, and the truck didn't stop. In fact, it sped up. Frankie panicked, shouting at me to let go and jump, which he did. Now it was my turn, but Frankie's fear had paralyzed me. I didn't think I could let go.

I woke up in an ambulance about a block from my father's farm. My mother never found out.

The summer ended not long after that. My father's vegetable plants died. We went back to school, where the teacher told me that my shirt was the whitest she'd ever seen, and that my mother must work very hard. I didn't know what to say in response.

Before long the grass in the parks was frozen in the morning, and we went back to the waste barrels on Arthur Avenue to get food for the rabbits, separating out the parsley and the celery–except for Jimmy, who shouted as he shoved the bad food in, "But when are these rabbits gonna die?"

Christmas morning, Frankie woke up under the stove as usual. I think he liked being out in the kitchen where he could look at the little Christmas tree on the table. Frank and I had taken to decorating it ourselves by this time, because Ma was so busy with Catherine and the housework. We had saved up pennies to buy bulbs for the old string of lights.

Compa' Joe and *Zi'* Nettie came for coffee in the afternoon, bringing a newspaper and a dish of cookies. With the coffee my mother put out a little bottle of Anisette that she had made herself. The grownups played cards and told old stories in Italian. The radio was on; my mother sang along with the songs she knew, sometimes getting the others to join in. She set the table with a saucer under every cup, as she learned to do in Bisaccia, when she was a girl and her sister was married to the mayor. The smell of the black Italian coffee and the sweet anisette filled the apartment.

We brothers had to leave one cookie for Catherine, and then we looked at the paper and the funnies. I saved articles for my scrapbook, with titles like, "Mayor Puts a Ban on Artichoke Sales to Curb Rackets" and "Five Nations Promise War Aid to Britain if Italians Attack." The War article might go next to a photo of Mussolini. The artichoke article, with its photo of Mayor LaGuardia making a speech from the back of a truck at the Bronx Terminal Market, and policemen in the background blowing bugles, might get a place of honor.

That year was the first that I remember going to gather old Christmas trees near the farm, a few days after the holiday. As we walked, we passed pile after pile of trees that people had dragged out of their apartments and left for the garbage men. There must have been hundreds.

My father walked with us. "Look," he said, "I use these for tomatoes. *Li portat'a* farm, eh?" And then he went to work. He didn't say how many trees to gather, or what the old trees had to do with tomatoes, but Augie and Jimmy seemed to know what to do. Frankie and I followed without saying a word.

Augie made sure to drag his first tree close by a bunch of boys hanging around on the sidewalk. "Miele, what are you doing?" one of them yelled.

"Gotta make a pile of these trees at my father's farm. We're gonna burn 'em!"

"Yeah? Can I help?"

"Can I help?"

"Can I help?"

"Sure," Augie said, and he led them, all dragging trees, to where Pop wanted us to pile them at the farm. It became a competition to see who could gather the most. Before long, we had cleared all the piles for blocks around.

After my father got home from work, we helped him to burn the trees. The dried needles and dead branches made a fast fire that flared up high; that was the fun for us boys in the wintertime, watching the big flames jump into the sky. After the fire died down, we cut away what remained of the branches and piled up the trunks, which were full of sap and didn't burn as fast. Those would be stakes for the tomatoes.

The stakes would support hundreds of tomatoes next summer. My father always sold the best ones, but saved the rest for my mother to can for the endless pots of tomato gravy. Those pots of gravy got our family through the Great Depression in New York City. We made whatever we could, fixed whatever got broken, spent money only on the necessities. We brothers each had only the basics in clothing. We never had pasta from a box; it was too expensive. And if the chickens didn't lay eggs, we did without; who was going to pay for eggs at the store? Ma only bought meat when we didn't have enough chicken or rabbit meat from the farm, and even then, we only got the least expensive cuts. When there was no meat, we ate beans with pasta, *pasta fagioli*, sometimes for days or weeks on end.

Eleanor Roosevelt pronounced it "pastafazool" on the radio one day: "A family of four can dine on pastafazool, a healthy and hearty dish, for only fifteen cents a day." My mother cussed her and called her *"denti cavall'*," horse teeth. She didn't like the president's wife, who was dining on anything she wanted, telling us that we were all right because we had plenty of "pastafazool".

***

We learned to find our own way. We learned what a dollar was worth: 50 shopping bags, 20 shoe shines. A shoe shine would buy two slices of cake with a little left over for a cup of coffee to share, and 40 shoe shines got you a pair of sneakers.

Would we have been happier if we had been given every comfort? I don't know. I know a man who grew up an orphan, but slept in a warm bed, got fed and clothed, had toys, trips, games, and a chance to do his school work every night. He always seemed unhappy, even when he had left childhood behind. I woke up cold in the winter as a child, and wore sneakers with holes in the snow. Our breakfast was stale bread every day. The only thing that changed was that we dumped it in coffee, or tea, or Ovaltine, or milk, if we could get it. I didn't even own a coat. My parents couldn't give those things to me.

But we were happy. I don't know if we could have been happier otherwise, and I don't think it really matters.

My parents did not have the money to give us much in the way of material necessities, but instead they gave us something that no one can buy: the spirit we needed to survive in hard times and to enjoy what we had.

You can't dwell on hardship or on mistakes. You learn from them. You learn from the past, and you live for the future.

I couldn't have spoken these words at age seven, but I was able to face an uncertain manhood on the streets of the Bronx because my parents instilled in me a belief in hard work. As I came of age in the 1930s, America left the Depression behind. But we young immigrants from the ghettoes, steeped in family values and prepared for lives of manual labor, were poorly prepared for World War II. The draft was about to come in, reminding us, for better or worse, that we owed our lives to America.

ARMAND MILLE

ROCKLAND
COUNTY TIMES weekly

Above Right:
High-School graduation,
June 1947

Above Left:
In uniform 1951

Left:
With the unit at
Camp Roberts, Indiana

The Draft

American Dreams Promised and Lost

In 1943, the summer after I turned 14, I worked for Tank Levsky, one of the Kosher butchers on Kingsbridge Road. The Jewish neighborhood was the only place to get a job in a store; Arthur Avenue was still all pushcarts. I had started with Tank at age 11, as a delivery boy, and moved up to working the counter. I did whatever I was asked, even plucking the chickens. The lice were unbelievable! I learned to work fast so they wouldn't get into my clothes, but some Friday afternoons I still came home scratching. Tank Levsky liked me because I was polite with the customers, and could add the prices in my head quickly, without making a mistake.

After the Japanese attacked Pearl Harbor, the draft took all the working-age young men from the neighborhood, and my brothers and I became little men. We did men's work, for kids' pay. Augie and Jimmy started delivering ice and moving furniture even before dropping out of school at 16. Jimmy drove a moving truck, sometimes even out of state, and supervised loading and unloading. I helped my brothers on a few occasions. I remember moving a piano with Augie once. He put his shoulders underneath his side, and I did the same on my side.

"On three, Armand," he said, "Okay? One, two... three!" and we lifted.

As soon as I was up I sank to my knees. But somehow we got it where it needed to go. We were men before our time. We came home with real money now, not handfuls of nickels.

When Frank and I were not in school or working, we hung out with Joe DiGuardi, who worked at the fruit store down the street from Tank Levsky's. Joe liked to go to the gym and hang out with the boxers, so Frankie and I went along too.

I could fight, but not like Frank. He had the biggest heart a person could have and backed it up with his long, strong arms. He always found trouble, defending his family and friends, because he loved to fight, rarely lost, and didn't care if his so-called friends were using him to fight their battles. Fighting to him was the same as someone else eating a plate of pasta — part of a normal, satisfying day.

In junior high, I saw him fight with a broken foot and win. We were walking to school, with Frankie on his crutches, when he caught sight of a guy who had made trouble for a friend of his. The jerk started to pick on Frankie. "Well, if it ain't Hopalong!"

Hopalong was the name of a cowboy movie character in those days. The movies were popular, but the kid wasn't paying Frankie a compliment.

"I gotta get him," Frankie said to me.

"Are you nuts?" I said. But I saw the look in his eye; he couldn't just walk by this guy. I said, "Frank, I'll do it. Let me fight him."

"Get outta here," Frank growled, and he threw his crutches at me. He hopped right up to the other guy and called him out. They circled each other for only a few seconds before it was all over. One, two. The other guy went down. Frank hopped back over to me, picked up his crutches with a big, beautiful smile, and we went to school.

Frankie soon became a local celebrity as an amateur boxer. Somewhere, maybe because of the kid who called him "Hopalong", he got the idea of wearing a toy gun belt when he entered the ring. They called him "Two-Gun Miele." On the street they called him "Shorty," but with great respect. He could knock down any of these so-called tough guys, no matter how big. Like I said, he had long arms. And a big, big heart.

***

In September, I started my first year at Theodore Roosevelt High School. Frankie planned to quit in October when he turned 16, just as Augie and Jimmy had.

My brothers didn't quit school because they had no brains. We all did well in school, and were considered bright. But high school did not allow enough time for work. It was the same for all the young men in the neighborhood. Work came first, because of the feeling of responsibility for the family. Most everyone I knew was strictly blue-collar.

I began to wonder, though. Why shouldn't I be able to work in a suit, like a gentleman? Why shouldn't I graduate high school?

I'd been a straight-A student all through junior high, even though I could never study at home. I got my homework done in the time before classes started at school, or during lunch or recess. I never took a book home, but kept up somehow. One time, a teacher assigned "Moby Dick". I wouldn't have minded reading it, but I couldn't; I worked all afternoon, and in the evening after dinner, Pop turned off all the lights. So when I came to school each day, I asked the other students about the assigned chapters. I got a good score on the exam, just from hearing about the book from others. I scored higher than another boy who, would you believe, raised his hand and asked the teacher, "Why did Miele get a higher score than me? He didn't even read the book!"

The teacher told him, "If he got a higher score than you without even reading the book, you've really got a problem!"

And so it went. I always got by, and even did well.

But in my first week at Theodore Roosevelt High I began to run into problems.

One morning in my economics class, the teacher, Mr. Small, started to speak about politics. He loved Franklin Roosevelt. "Your families should thank this great man for leading our country into the future, and vote for him for another presidential term."

I thought, this man is campaigning, not teaching economics. This is not what I am here to learn.

I had my own ideas about Franklin Roosevelt. Because I was good at math, I'd been doing my father's taxes every year. I knew how hard he and my brothers worked. On the forms I saw that Roosevelt was taxing some people to 91 percent of their income. Even my father, who only made a few thousand dollars a year, was expected to pay 20 percent of it in income taxes. So I had my reasons for doubting FDR's handling of the economy, even as a high school kid.

I also felt that Roosevelt had kept us in the War. I read the papers avidly, as young as I was, and I thought that for the teacher to just give one side of things was not right. If he was going to talk about Franklin Roosevelt, he should talk about Thomas Dewey too, and about Wendell Wilkie, whose campaign caravan drove right down Arthur Avenue this summer. Was Franklin Roosevelt coming to the Bronx for our votes? I didn't think so.

I might have been young, but I insisted on being heard — an attitude that stood me in good stead all my life.

So I stood up and told Mr. Small, "If we are going to talk politics, I would like to give my view."

He shouted at me to sit down.

I'd learned to show my teachers respect, so I didn't shout back, but I didn't sit down right away. "I don't think Roosevelt is great," I insisted.

One of the other boys jumped up now. "You'd better take that back!" he yelled.

"I said sit down, Mr. Miele," Mr. Small said.

"What about him?" I said, pointing to the other guy.

Mr. Small pointed at me. "You'd better worry about yourself, sir," he boomed.

"Roosevelt is not great!" I repeated.

Now the other student jumped me. A fight broke out. Most of the students seemed to think like the teacher, but some joined in to help me, and it became a brawl. Mr. Small ran out in the hall where he saw the gym teacher passing by, and called him in to break it up.

I thought it was on the street that I'd fight all my battles, and that fighting was something a man did with his fists, but I learned something different during my time at Theodore Roosevelt High School.

After the first trouble with Mr. Small, every economics test I took received a barely-passing mark. I answered all the questions right, but he graded me low on my writing. When I asked him why I got a low mark on one test, he ridiculed me by reading my writing aloud in a mocking way, making the other students laugh.

I thought it was my imagination, but it seemed that certain other teachers also refused to grade my work well. In my homeroom, there was a girl who had a few classes with me, including economics. She always asked me about the homework, and she copied all my notes. She got A's while I just passed. I couldn't understand how I could be working so hard and getting such low marks. For the first time I gave up working after school so that I could study.

After midterms, I became convinced that Mr. Small wanted me to fail. There was a student sitting behind me who had been in the Armed Services, but left, for whatever reason. We took our midterm exam. Afterwards, he was all upset; he was sure he'd failed. Mr. Small told him not to get excited, that he'd gotten one of the highest marks in the class.

He tapped me on the shoulder. "Miele!" he said. "I must talk to you."

I'd never had a conversation with this person, and I wondered why he so urgently wanted to talk to me. When he was able to take me aside, he told me, "Miele, if I got one of the highest marks, you definitely had to have got the highest. I copied everything over your shoulder."

Guess what—I got one of the lowest marks in the class. That's right. Mr. Small was a phony. As winter came on, I began to wonder whether it was worth it to struggle so hard.

***

For once, I was not looking forward to Christmas. Augie had been drafted into the Navy, and Jimmy volunteered, although he was only 17. He knew the draft was going to get him in a year anyway, and he figured that he could at least avoid the Army; the Navy, he said, was a cleaner operation. As I've said, he didn't like getting dirty. Yet Augie and Jimmy weren't unhappy. They were going to serve their country, and that commanded a lot of respect from people. They were finally being treated like the men they were.

Frankie was happy too. He had quit school for good once he turned 16. He had two years before the draft would get him, and hoped that by the then the War would be over. He'd been going to the gym a lot with Joe DiGuardi, beating a lot of local boxers and making a little extra money. He put the money into getting a bigger Christmas tree this year. This one reached almost to the ceiling from the little table it stood on. He dressed it with a new string of lights. Underneath it he put Ma's Christmas present, a new coffee set with saucers, cups, and even matching teaspoons. He had to borrow a little from me to pay for it, which I knew he'd forget to pay back, but I didn't mind. I was so glad he remembered to get Ma a present.

I seemed to be the only one who felt bad. I was angry about school and lonely because my brothers were growing away from the family. As things got harder at school, I'd seen Frankie and Joe less and less. The economics midterm left me feeling the odds against my graduating like a lead weight. What if I did all this work only to get left behind, either by failing to graduate or by getting drafted? Maybe I should give up school and build my life on the honest, hard work of my back, like my father did, like my brothers were doing.

Frankie urged me to come with him to the gym one Saturday afternoon, a couple of weeks before Christmas, just a few days before my birthday, in fact. He was going to fight one of his rivals. He'd beaten him before, but the other guy had also beaten Frank. It was the kind of thing Frank loved. He couldn't wait.

We got to the gym to find a crowd not just around the ring, but spilling out the door, with Joe DiGuardi squeezing through to meet us. "Armand! How you been? How's-a-the-Eengleesh-a?"

We all laughed. That was Joe's way of asking about school. A lot of the guys joked with me about quitting work to stay in school, "learning to talk good." Some were not so nice about it, and I had to use my fists to make them back off, but Joe meant well.

"Come on, we'll be in Frank's corner."

Frankie put on his shorts and his gun belt. Joe and I made sure Frank had water, a couple of towels. The spectators were already getting loud.

Frank and his opponent fought well, and the guys watching were having a great time. There were cheers for both fighters, whenever one of them got in a shot. But I wasn't having a good time. It's like for the first time, I saw my brother getting hit, and getting hurt.

Frank had been in a million fights, like I've said, and at first, he gave as good as he got. But it was a long match, and it began to take its toll.

A minute into the final round, Frank landed his famous left hook. The other guy staggered backward three steps but did not go down.

"The right, Frank, the right!" Joe and I screamed. "Finish him!"

Frank was moving much slower now. He didn't get in quick to follow up, almost looked like he was waiting for the other guy to come back. In fact, Frank practically stepped into the next shot, a right hook that landed hard on his ear.

"Don't let him get you, Frank!" Joe yelled. "Uppercut!"

Joe was right; the other guy was not guarding himself well, and was open to a shot to the jaw. But Frank was still lurching sideways, with a look on his face like he was wondering what to do next. The other guy moved forward. Frank didn't look like he could meet him. At that moment, I couldn't stand to see my brother go down.

A folding chair went flying into the ring, narrowly missing the other guy's head.

Did I throw that? I thought.

Suddenly I was in the ring, scrambling for Frank's opponent, while around me everyone in the gym went crazy. I heard Frank behind me, talking around the mouthguard. "Armand, what are you doing?"

At the same time, I'm yelling. "You get off my brother!"

The other guy backed off right away, and someone grabbed me. Luckily I looked around before I swung at him. It was Joe.

***

After the riot I caused, the boxing match broke up and the police had to clear everyone out of the gym. At least Frankie didn't lose. But I was still all steamed up, and left to walk home alone while Joe and Frank worked things out with the other boxer.

I had a lot to think about, walking the half-mile home. My two oldest brothers leaving to serve in the Navy. Frank out of school. Me, struggling to fit into the mainstream society at Roosevelt, where I had the strong impression I wasn't wanted. By the time I reached my block, it wasn't yet dinnertime, but I had a new plan. I decided it was time to be a man.

I'd heard that there was work in Bridgeport, Connecticut, putting together submarines or pieces of submarines for the Navy, 90 miles away. I had a little pocket money, but a luxury like a train ticket didn't make sense for such a short trip. I could probably hitchhike it by nightfall. I'd have to swing a job at the submarine factory within the week, before my money ran out.

No matter if the president was keeping us in the War. I was an American, and I wanted to do my part. I was tired of waiting. I pulled my jacket up under my chin, yanked my hat down over my ears, shoved my hands in my pockets, and headed for the Bronx River Parkway.

By dark, I'd just gotten out of the city, and was hitchhiking along the Merritt Parkway, when a police car pulled up. The cop asked where I was from and where I was going. "I'm from the Bronx," I told him, "and I'm going to work on defense." But when he asked my age I had to tell him I was 14 years old. Within minutes he'd flagged down a passing car with New York plates, and instructed the man driving to bring me back to the Bronx. I was too cold to say anything on the way back. I put my stiff, frozen hands between my knees and tried hard to keep from shivering. I guessed I'd just have to wait.

I'll never forget the look on my mother's face when I finally walked in the apartment, long after dark. She'd kept the dinner waiting for me.

***

It was my big brother Augie that kept me going after midterms.

Christmas Day, we'd just finished dinner, and Ma was getting the coffee ready, all excited over Frank's new coffee set. The rest of the family got out the pack of cards.

Augie got up from the table. "Come on, Armand, I've got something for you."

He led me to the bedroom and opened the closet. He pulled out the most beautiful white button-down shirt, the kind you'd see a guy wear with a fancy suit in a movie, someone like Clark Gable or Gary Cooper. A gentleman's shirt.

"I got this for going dancing on Friday nights," he told me, holding it out. "Merry Christmas, little brother!"

"Geez, Augie," was all I could think to say. I didn't even have a suit to wear it with.

But it reminded me of what I was thinking when school started, before Mr. Small's midterm, that maybe I could do this, I could graduate high school and work like a gentleman. I hung the shirt in my closet. I decided I'd go back to school–to see if I could make it for just one more day.

***

I made it for a lot more than the day. I received my diploma in June of 1947.

On graduation day, I was at the ceremonies with all my classmates, wearing Augie's shirt and a borrowed suit, proud of what I'd accomplished, and excited about beginning a new life. The draft was still in the back of my mind. Frank had just gotten drafted into the Army, even though the War was over. They needed men to work in the aftermath. Nobody liked the draft, but during the War you tolerated it. Now, two years after the War ended, the draft was still on and I began to wonder what excuse the government would use next to extend it.

Still, our family was lucky. Augie and Jimmy had both gotten shipped to the Philippines, where Augie worked as a ship's mechanic. Jimmy was with an amphibious assault operation, responsible for piloting the boat that transported the troops from ship to shore. Both escaped injury. Now they were back in the Bronx after serving their time, and Augie would soon be married.

Who should approach me at the graduation ceremony but the gym teacher who broke up the fight in my economics class so long ago. He came to congratulate me with tears in his eyes.

Why is he crying? I wondered.

"What's the problem?" I asked. "Are you okay?"

"I thought you would never leave this school with a diploma. You've got to be someone special."

I thanked him, but I didn't really understand. What was he so surprised about?

It wasn't until 1953, after reading an article in "Time", that I found out the New York City teacher's union was home to one of the biggest underground communist organizations in America in the 1940s. I believe I was targeted that first day of school, when I spoke against Franklin Roosevelt in my economics class. My hard work, and the work of many other students like me, was rewarded with low marks and ridicule, because the teachers had political agendas and wanted kids who thought differently to get disgusted and quit school. Many students did quit under the pressure.

We were just kids. What did they think we'd be able to do?

Similar things go on in our schools and other organizations. Things are so one-sided and extreme these days, you can imagine our country being overrun one day by people who take away our freedoms without firing a shot.

***

I left the apartment early one morning not long after graduation, dressed in my borrowed suit. I had the newspaper classifieds under my arm, a pencil in my pocket, and my diploma, carefully tucked into the newspaper. I'd circled every ad that read, "Recent High School Graduate, No Experience Necessary." I walked to the station to save a nickel on bus fare, and took the subway to Manhattan.

I might as well have been crossing the ocean. Although the Bronx is a part of New York City, it seemed like a different country that day. There were no grocers in the first neighborhood I visited, no pushcarts, just the office workers, all dressed in suits and walking fast to get to their jobs in buildings well over 10 stories high. I studied the classifieds and approached one of these buildings.

I found the elevator and took a speedy ride up to the twelfth floor. Whoosh. Then I located the right door: "J.K. Smit & Co., Fine Industrial Tools." The receptionist looked at me with a sour face, as if my suit jacket was full of holes. She wasn't interested in my diploma.

"I'm sorry," she interrupted me. "We just filled that position."

In another office, in another gigantic building, I got the same treatment. The excuse this time was, "That position no longer exists."

In what I suppose was the most honest encounter that day, the boss himself told me, not in an unfriendly way, "Look, son, this is Manhattan. I can't put an Italian at the front desk. I'm sorry. Best of luck, though."

Diploma in hand, I was still a "Guinea", a "WOP", or a "dago." This was 1947; we didn't talk about "discrimination." In my mind, I just didn't mix with the normal population.

I wanted to toss my diploma in the garbage along with the classifieds, when I found out how useless it was, but I kept it. My mother had been bragging to all her friends about me graduating. I would have to go back to work with my father, as a laborer, but I knew my mother wouldn't want me to throw away my diploma.

My father got me a job as a concrete laborer. I mixed yards and yards of concrete by hand, and dug ditches deep and long. I came home dead tired. I was a good worker. The boss gave me more and more responsibility until I was working as a mason, a professional tradesman.

I still got the pay of a laborer though, because I didn't have a union card. You had to inherit your union membership or get it by being hired to a union job (a "Catch-22", because only union members got hired for union jobs). But I didn't care. I felt I had at least developed the skill to get me moving up the ladder.

Over the next two years, I learned a trade and became proud of it.

***

At age 19, I went through a period when I couldn't get a job, so I started a business on my own for the first time. This came about with the help of my brother Augie. He liked working as a mechanic during the War, and had gotten a lot of that type of work since he got back. He knew all the junk men, through dealing with them to get used parts.

During this dry period, I started running errands for Augie. I became friendly with one of the junk shop owners, and visited the place at times, looking for good deals. One day I saw a dump truck, junked for scrap: no headlights, no tires, in bad shape. But I loved it. I asked if I could buy it, and I swung my first big deal. I paid $75 cash, and was permitted to remove any parts I needed from the other junked trucks in the yard. With some hard work, Augie's help, a fresh coat of paint, and lots of heart I was on my way. I was in business.

My first job was to clean out the basement of a local church. I didn't charge to clean out the basement. Instead, I made my profit by selling the old chairs, desks, or anything that had some value to the people in the neighborhood. They could use almost anything, even if it needed repairs. Selling off that first load put my business in the black.

Soon I got more jobs and could hire workers. I became important among my friends, who looked forward to getting some work from me. My men and I began to take on jobs in cement work and in excavation, digging everything by hand.

One of my regular guys was Mackie, an acquaintance of my father's, a widower, who'd been involved in construction contracting for a long time. He'd worked for a lot of the bosses, and had seen how things were done. He took an interest in me and gave me good advice on handling the business.

Soon we were getting jobs all over the Bronx. We installed and insulated a boiler, which involved concrete work. We also got a subcontract on a New York City job, digging new sewer lines. This was a big deal for a small firm like mine.

Mackie never asked, but when I could afford it I gave him a cut of the profits. Believe me, it wasn't much, but he appreciated it. Even more, he appreciated having the chance to put his know-how to work, and he most enjoyed joining us for my mother's home-cooked meals. He became almost like one of the family.

Mackie was closer to my father's age than mine, though. Maybe even older. He died suddenly one winter, alone in his own apartment.

I'd known old people who died before, and it never bothered me much; after all, I always thought, it was sad, but they were old and their time had come. When Mackie died, I was taken by surprise at the feeling of loss. He taught me everything he knew, and now I was on my own.

At the time, I had four or five jobs going. I was 21 years old, with 23 men working for me. I had a successful business, and I had a name. I didn't see much money, though; I took from Peter to pay Paul, so that between paying the bills and paying the men, not to mention the jobs that didn't pay right away, or at all, there was never much left. I wondered how to continue the business on my own.

Could I do less hiring? Maybe. But how could I let these men down? These immigrant workers, men with three or four or more children, friends of my father, who came to my parents' apartment after dinner, asking, "Does your son have a job for me?"

And my father. I couldn't let him down either. He sat down with the men one at a time, as proud as can be of me, the youngest of his boys. He'd tell these men, "I will talk to my son."

With Mackie's help, I'd gained some knowledge of construction. I knew the language to use to get work. I was good in math, and could put together fair estimates to get the jobs. Most of all, I'd known the men who were my employees all my life. They lived to work. They were proud. To apply for welfare would be a disgrace to them and to their families. I took jobs to keep them working, even when there would be no profit, even when the work was digging sewers in the winter by hand. I was able to keep almost two dozen hard-working men employed for two years after Mackie died.

Then something happened to interfere with my going business, something I couldn't resist. I received my "greetings" from the United States Army.

***

This was 1951, not too long after the "Great War," World War II. President Truman's "police action" in Korea had begun the summer before. Truman's administration told our soldiers that all they had to do was show their weapons, and the North Koreans would retreat back across the 38th Parallel. The Koreans responded with Chinese tanks and machine guns. The Americans, carrying only limited artillery and basic survival supplies, were outmatched. Hundreds of soldiers and civilians were taken prisoner right off the bat.

My belief now is that Korea was a phony war, a way to create jobs during a time that the government feared another Great Depression. The country spent itself out funding World War II. All the resources went into war manufacturing; there was nothing left for domestic needs like new housing. Rationing of basics like sugar, coffee, and gas had brought about a huge black market.

The new veterans had no work to come home to. They mostly belonged to the "52-20" club. The government would give them $20 a week for a year. Like it or not, this is what most of them had to live on, and even in those days, $20 a week was not much. The Korean War created new jobs for these men in war manufacturing at home; and some of them went back into the service.

The true heroes of Korea were the poor guys who lost their limbs and their lives, their minds and their souls, fighting for their country. Two weeks was as long as the first soldiers were supposed to be over there. Instead, aside from the many who were wounded or killed, thousands more were captured, and many hundreds of those were held prisoner for years. To this day, hundreds of American prisoners, taken at the outset of the Korean War, have not been accounted for. Why were they sent in such a hurry? What was Truman trying to prove, and what were he and his cronies getting out of it?

On the newsreels and in "Time", we saw the new draftees in the Korean winter, not properly prepared. They wrapped newspapers around their legs in the sub-zero cold, and many came home frostbitten. The prisoners, I guess, didn't even have the benefit of newspapers; we didn't see pictures of them at all. They were lost somewhere in that bitter enemy winter. More prisoners were taken. Often our soldiers couldn't return the enemy's fire, because their guns were frozen.

I was drafted to the Korean War not long after Christmas of 1951. When I got my conscription letter I thought back to the winter after I turned 15, when Augie and Jimmy went to the Navy. My brothers each did their time, so I guessed it was my turn. But I was doing my country a lot more good at home than I could ever do fighting in Korea.

Families depended on me to pave the way for more jobs, and to collect the money they'd earned. I tried to get a 30-day deferment, to complete the jobs I'd started and make my collections. It didn't happen, even though I hired a lawyer for the purpose. Who knows whether he even did anything. Lawyers always have excuses. In the end, the government couldn't even give me 30 days. It was a bitter disappointment.

The night before I left, there was a big party at my parents' apartment to send me off. The smell of Ma's strong espresso and homemade anisette warmed the living room, and the radio played Dean Martin. Augie and Jimmy's little girls played with their dolls and sang along with Ma's broken English to the songs on the radio.

I was angry. I should have been anxious or fearful, maybe, worrying about what army life would be like, or the sub-zero winter in Korea; I should have been sad that I wouldn't smell Ma's anisette for a long time, and that my nieces would no longer be little girls in two years. But instead, I was angry. I was mostly concerned with losing my business.

I'd invited an accountant to the party. For the first time, I'd hired a professional to arrange my affairs. He remarked, "How did a kid like you amass this money and such a big contracting business?"

I thought, who is he kidding?

He couldn't believe that a 23-year-old could have done what I did, starting from nothing but a broken-down truck with a new coat of paint. Well, I did it.

So what, I thought, now it will all be gone.

I left everything to Jimmy. He seemed worried about whether he could handle it, since he was married and had a child. He couldn't put the business and his workers first, as I did. But there was no one else who could take charge. Augie already ran his own garage.

"Look," I said to him, "Everything is yours. I'm taking twenty-five dollars." I showed him the collections to be made, and the jobs to be finished. "The only thing I ask in return is that when I get back, if the business is still operating, that I can be a full partner."

Four o'clock the next morning, I took the subway to Whitehall Street. From there I boarded a train to Fort Devins in Massachusetts.

***

I was cold in my civilian clothes. I'd left my old coat with Frankie, thinking I'd soon get a new one from the Army.

Two years, I thought. Two years to serve my country, that's all. My brothers had done it, and it was right that I should do it too.

That first night on the train, I woke to the sound of crying, and it was loud. Poor guys. A lot of them had never been on their own, and they were scared. They already missed their families, their girlfriends, and their homes.

In the morning, we disembarked and were driven in buses to Devins, a cold collection of barracks buildings. Here we were injected against diseases and given very short haircuts. Then we were issued our uniforms. I now felt comfortable in this mean cold weather. We took exams for one solid week, so that the Army would know what we were qualified for. I was assigned to Camp Roberts, California, for infantry training. This, at least, was something to be excited about. I was going to see the country.

The night before I left for California, I stood in a fast-moving line, the fastest I ever stood on in the Army. At the front of the line, an officer gave us $10 each, which we called "the Flying Ten," because it never stayed in anyone's pocket long.

Back in the barracks, a fellow came to me and said in a soft voice, "I know some of the same people that you know in the neighborhood." He was scared. He asked me to watch out for him. But you know what, I never saw him again. That was the beginning of army life.

***

California here I come! I'd never made a trip more than an hour from home before, let alone across the whole country on a train. Back in the Bronx, the only open spaces were the vacant lots in between buildings, or the places that no one could build on. I had seen deserts and prairies in the movies, but I didn't believe there could be so much space until I left on that train to California. For seven straight days I looked out the window in amazement. The mountains were tremendous and the deserts like waste spaces.

We had a stopover in Los Angeles, and a bunch of us decided to visit the bars near the train station. We were from New York, remember, so we thought we knew it all. Outside the bars, girls were coming up to us, saying, "How about a drink, soldier?"

I thought, why not? I had $10, after all, and I was a soldier now. The ex-GI's I knew in New York had told me about places like these, hadn't they? It seemed a friendly enough atmosphere.

I paired up with a guy from the train, Andy D., who I'd just met. We went in one place and ordered a beer, but the bartender said, "We don't serve Indians!"

I started to get hot under the collar, but Andy tugged my sleeve. "Not you," he said. "But I am an Indian. This happens all the time."

Outside, he thanked me for wanting to stand up for him, but said it wasn't worth it to cause trouble. He just went back and waited for the rest of us on the train.

So I ended up going into the next place alone. This time, as I ordered a beer for myself, a young lady approached and asked if I'd buy her a drink. Why not! I'd learned, of course, that you never let a lady pay. And it was only a one-hour stopover. My ten should last at least that long.

She ordered a whisky of some sort. We chatted a little, and she ordered another. This time I thought, something's wrong. I hadn't even finished my beer. I picked up her drink and tasted it. It was only tea.

When I got angry and confronted her, she made a signal to the bartender, and that was it. Without saying a word, the bartender pulled a gun from under the counter and pointed it at me. It looked bigger than John Wayne's Colt .45. I got out of there fast.

And that was the end of the Flying Ten.

***

My experiences as a soldier among civilians didn't get much better. There wasn't a lot of respect for the uniform; in fact, more the opposite, as I soon found out. To make matters worse, to our higher-ups in the Army, us draftees were the lowest of the low.

After a lot of orientation and more paperwork, I got sent to Fort Lewis, Washington, for basic training. The officers in charge didn't know much more than us draftees. They tried to cover it up by treating us like kids.

The so-called discipline began with bunk inspections. We got bossed around and yelled at for things like having a wrinkle in the blanket, or forgetting to say "sir." I didn't let this bother me at first, because I saw that this was the Army's way of getting us used to following orders and behaving like soldiers. But I was a business owner in New York, a responsible worker, a man. I never became comfortable calling someone "sir" who had not earned my respect.

After the first phase of battle training, which they called a "bivouac", I knew that none of these guys would ever earn my respect. It was a fiasco. These officers were supposed to lead us into battle, and I saw them doing such stupid things that I knew once the real thing started we'd have no chance. They got units mixed up, to begin with, because they couldn't read maps well enough to figure out where everyone's locations were supposed to be. Instead of functioning as units, we became just a bunch of bewildered guys bumping into each other.

The guys in charge had blinkers on. They never saw anyone coming from behind and didn't know how to protect themselves. If I have to follow these guys into battle, I thought, I'm doomed along with the rest of my unit. With these new experiences to reflect on, I hitchhiked into Seattle on my first day off. I went into a diner to order a cup of coffee, just so I could sit and think on my own.

The waitress served the guy right next to me like I wasn't even there. I tried to get her attention, but she just turned away. Finally, I said, "Miss, I'd like a cup of coffee."

"I don't serve soldiers," she said.

I tried to laugh it off. "That's a nice joke, but I'd like a cup of coffee, please."

She gave me a look and said again, "I don't serve soldiers."

I was furious. "You bitch," I said. "You get me a cup of coffee right now."

She got the coffee without another word, but she also ran and got three goons from the back room. They were cab drivers or something, rough-looking guys with straps around the bottoms of their pants legs. They surrounded me. "You're gonna pay for that coffee and get out of here, soldier, or you're gonna die."

I picked up my fork, holding it like a knife, and turned to face them. "You want it that way, fine," I said, "But one of you is coming with me."

They backed off. But then they called the police. At least I got to finish my coffee while we waited.

I couldn't believe that this nice-looking waitress and these ragged cab drivers were all on the same team. Yet it was the cop who disgusted me the most.

He came and settled everyone down, and I went with him out to the sidewalk. He didn't arrest me. He said he was sorry to have to remove me.

"I was in World War II, son, and I been through that too," he said, nodding his head toward the diner.

"You were in World War II? And you're with them?"

He didn't say anything. I'd gotten my coffee, I don't even think I paid for it, and I'd gotten myself under control. I don't want to be arrested, I told myself. But I was shaking.

I said, "How dare you? How in hell did you become a cop?"

"That's enough, soldier," he said, but he didn't threaten me. "I'm trying to help you out. Now go on and get out of here."

The coffee felt like poison in my stomach. I thought again about the business back home, about my good reputation as a boss and a worker. Now that I was in the Army, all I struggled for my whole life had become worthless.

I got a ride back to camp, so I was able to walk in well before curfew. But there were low-level officers just above us draftees, MPs and sergeants and corporals, who lived to bust the draftees' balls. They really weren't any better than the civilians in the diner. They were scared, maybe, or maybe just pumped up over the little bit of power they had, remembering how they were treated when they first enlisted or got drafted.

An Army jeep zoomed up and nearly hit me walking into camp. "What the hell!" I yelled at the MP driving.

Of course he and his buddy now stopped to give me the third degree.

"What are you doing out, soldier?" one of them shouted.

"I went out!" I said. "So what? I'm getting back before curfew."

"Don't tell me when curfew is, soldier!" he snapped. "Where's your ID? What were you doing?"

I got upset with them and said, "What the hell is your problem?"

For this, they kept me overnight in a cage. I'm not talking about a cell, with even a bench or a chair, but a cage in a cement room, like you'd see in a torture chamber.

They reported me to the lieutenant, who looked like a regular guy. He didn't come on strong, like the MPs and the others who liked to show off. He said, "Miele, the MPs might get a little rough, but they were just doing their jobs last night. Why wouldn't you discuss your whereabouts with them?"

I could see that it would only make more trouble to argue with the lieutenant, and anyway I had nothing to be ashamed of. I told him what happened in the diner.

He shook his head. He'd heard stories like this before. "I'm supposed to court-martial you for that kind of behavior, Miele. You can't threaten civilians," he said. "Do you have anything else to say about your encounter?"

"Yes, sir," I said. "Only that I could not allow them to insult this uniform."

He smiled a little, looking down at his papers.

"All right, Miele," he said. "You go on back to your duties for now. I'll let you know when your court-martial date is." But I never heard of a date; no one ever brought it up again.

I was beginning to learn the ropes in the Army. Like everywhere else, you just needed to make the right connections. Connections, as well as a huge coincidence, made the tide turn in my favor for a while.

My next time on leave, I was determined to get something out of my free trip west. I wanted to explore the coast from Seattle down to San Francisco by hitchhiking. I found a few soldiers from different companies to travel with.

We were all from the Bronx. We hitchhiked together and did a lot of talking about what was going on back home; all of us had different news, and fun memories of people we knew in common. One guy remembered a wedding we both went to, although we didn't know each other at the time.

He said, "The bride's brother is up here, too. He's a lieutenant."

That's right—he was talking about my unit's lieutenant.

So the next time I got in trouble, I was ready.

It was on my day off again. I was walking out the gate when a sergeant stopped me.

"Miele!" he yelled. I had to run back, naturally.

"Yes, sir."

"I want you to sweep my office before you leave the camp."

"It's my day off, sir." Same old song. These guys thought who the hell they were.

The sergeant pulled rank, of course. "Are you refusing my order, Miele? I want that office swept!"

"No, it's my day off!"

That was it. He ordered me to remain at camp for the rest of the day, and reported me. I was almost looking forward to it.

I reported to the lieutenant with a little smile. He must have thought I was crazy.

"Miele," he said. "In his report, the sergeant says that you refused his direct order Saturday morning. What do you say?"

"Sir," I said, "I don't know about that report. But I do know your brother-in-law. I went to his wedding on Tremont Avenue—"

And that was the end of the stupid bullying from the MPs and sergeants for me.

The lieutenant gave me a .45 and a Jeep, and it became my duty to pick up and deliver the payroll. Also, after finding out a bunch of us were from his wife's neighborhood back home, he took us down to North Beach in San Francisco to eat pasta. We got there late at night. The lieutenant had to bang on the door and holler up to a window, but the man inside was happy to cook for us once he was up.

After the lieutenant saw that I did well with the responsibility of the payroll, and got to know me better, his favorable reports on me paid off. The Army sent me to school in Indiana for training as an officer's aide.

On the day before I left for Indianapolis, I passed a corporal walking through camp. I'd gone a few yards past him when he yelled after me. "Miele! Get back here!"

I ran back. "What? What is it?" I asked, thinking there was something wrong.

He pointed to the ground at his feet. "Pick up that butt." A cigarette butt, and an old one at that. I hadn't even dropped it.

Instead of picking up the butt, I picked him up by the balls and threw him against a wall.

He never reported me.

***

I got to Camp Atterbury, Indiana in the summer of 1951, as the "police action" entered its second year. In the humid Midwestern heat, I thought how it must be in Korea, with the tropical rains as well as the heat. I was not sorry to be kept in the U.S.

I'm no coward, and I wasn't then. I just believed less and less in the Korean War. It had gotten worse. Truman had fired General MacArthur. The Chinese were involved openly now, supplying not just weapons, but also troops. There was no end in sight. We were being sent into chaos.

It looked like I would never set foot in Korea. Instead, I could hope to get something positive out of the Army. I had lost these months of my life, which I couldn't get back, but I still had 18 months to gain some skills, something I could use when I returned to my own world. I was eager to begin.

I started stenography classes as part of my new training, spending two hours a night at school. On Fridays, we got tested. If we didn't score 90 or above, we had to stay in classes all weekend too.

What made the schedule really rigorous was that I had to continue with daily basic training. I began to feel the pressure: I was unable to eat well and felt queasy during meals. I spat up a little blood once. But I didn't think anything of it. The same thing used to happen to me as a child, now and then, and it always went away.

The problems really started on a Saturday afternoon when I went with a buddy to a local dance. We got trouble from some civilian young men; that had become a matter of course. But we held our ground, the civilians backed off, and overall we had a good time, although we took a few hits.

We were on a bus back to camp when I felt an overwhelming urge to vomit. There was no warning; suddenly everything in my stomach wanted to come up. I hadn't even eaten anything. I snatched off my hat and threw up into it. It was all blood.

Afterwards, I felt just fine. No queasiness, nothing.

Back at camp, I cleaned out my hat and left it at my bunk. I went to the canteen for a soda, thinking to settle my stomach. A lot of guys were watching a boxing match on TV: Rocky Marciano versus Joe Louis. A great fight. I got my soda and tried to enjoy it with the other guys, but I suddenly felt sleepy. I went back to my bunk to lie down.

I woke up after dark, again feeling I had to throw up. I ran to the head. My vomit was all blood again. I found an old can and kept it next to my bed. Overnight, I spat up blood several more times.

At first light, feeling very weak now, I made my way to the medic's office. It was too early, though; no one was there, and it was locked up. But I had that urge to vomit again. I began to panic at the idea of spitting blood all over the steps there in public. I don't know how I found the strength, but I broke open the locked door.

I fell onto the floor of the waiting area, spewing blood everywhere. I found some towels in a closet and cleaned up the blood, or most of it. And then I passed out right there in the middle of the waiting room floor. I guess that's where they found me.

I was still recovering in bed when I got my medical discharge letter and $200 mustering-out pay. I wouldn't be permitted to finish my stenography class, let alone come back for the other classes. I stayed in the medic's care for another few days, and then got sent home.

I was at less than zero again. Six months of my life was lost, along with everything I had built up since graduating high school, and now I was too sick to work. I was born minus, and it seemed I'd never be able to catch up.

On my way back home, I had my last personal encounter with prejudice against soldiers.

Back in Indianapolis, I went to a bar to get a drink and a sandwich. The manager asked me to leave, pointing to a sign. It read, "No Dogs Allowed."

"I'm wearing this dog suit for you people, not for me," I told him, "And this is the way you treat me?"

But I didn't make any trouble. Maybe I was just feeling too sick. I left.

Waiting to board my train, I noticed three young men pointing at me and laughing. They were with a bunch of others on a line, you guessed it, boarding a train to an Army camp. Draftees.

"You have nothing to laugh at me about," I told them. "I'm going home."

It occurred to me that I was the one who should be laughing. They were just getting started in this mess. The poor jerks.

Above Left : With my
Buick Special, 1958

Above: My first
real estate office

Left: Gene
Crescenzi, a good
friend

The Suit

Gentlemen's Work

I came back to the Bronx a different person. I was sick and weak, still vomiting blood at times. The Army doctors had told me I had ulcers. The worst part, though, was that whereas I had left a strong, successful man, responsible for my family and for the families of my employees, I was now unable to even pay my keep at my parents' apartment. I was penniless and helpless.

Jimmy hadn't been able to keep the business going, and I couldn't blame him. He had his own life to lead and a family to raise. But I was the one who had the telegram from the Internal Revenue Service waiting for me when I got home. They wanted $400 that I owed in taxes, immediately.

The IRS was real friendly. They took my truck and most of my mustering-out pay, and called it even. Losing the truck was the worst part. To anyone else it was probably just a heap, but I felt that with the loss of that truck my last hopes of being able to start over were crushed.

I had worked so hard to build a business, and the very people I swore to fight and die for took it away from me. The same thing happened to young men all over the country. The draft hung over their heads, not allowing them to take on long-term responsibility. No one would hire a young man for fear he'd be sent overseas, and if he came back, he might not be competent to work.

Having nothing else, I tried to go back to what I knew. Cement. That spring I got jobs working alongside Frankie at construction sites once or twice, but I was just too weak. I couldn't go more than a couple of hours without nausea overtaking me. I was almost ashamed to take the few dollars the boss gave me for the couple of hours I worked on my last construction job. As I walked slowly home I thought about things. My mind was still sharp enough to work, even though the ulcers had weakened my body.

What could I do? Not hard labor. But I knew how to supervise and plan cement jobs, from my contracting experience. Maybe I could work as a tradesman and a supervisor, as a cement mason.

I'd never had a mason's union card, because the law was so twisted, but my skills qualified me to work as a mason. I'd read in the newspaper about the Taft-Hartley Act, and how Congress was using it to make new laws governing union rules. You still couldn't work a union job without a card; you couldn't get a union card without a union job. But if you were working a union job, they had to give you a union card.

There has to be a way to get a union job, I thought. I knew I was in for a fight, but the knowledge, if anything, settled my stomach a little for the first time in months.

The next day I went to the union hall to ask for a cement mason's union card. It was a long shot, but I thought it was worth it to ask. They knew me there. They had known me as a contractor. They knew me as a hard worker and an honest one. Could I take a test, pay extra dues, show a list of jobs I'd worked, get others to vouch for me? Why would they stop a reputable young man from working?

Well, the answers began with "Sorry," progressed through a million different excuses, and in the end it was, "No."

But I was prepared. Early the next morning I went to the biggest job in New York City, the construction of new city housing up past Pelham Parkway. I dressed in my mason's clothes, took my tools, and arrived before anyone else. I went to the masons' shed and sat on the bench to wait. It wasn't long before a person with a pencil behind his ear approached me. He asked for my name and union card.

"Armand Miele. I don't have a union card."

He looked puzzled. Who would show up to work without a union card? "Who sent you?"

"The big boss," I replied. "Who are you?"

"The shop steward," he said.

"Nice to meet you." That's all. I went back and sat on the same bench.

About 10 minutes later, another person, with a pencil behind his ear and a ruler in his pocket asked me, "Who sent you?"

"The big boss," I replied. He introduced himself as the foreman. "Nice to meet you," I said, and I waited a little longer. It was almost time go up to the floor where the masons were needed.

The third man to approach me had a pencil behind his ear, a ruler in his pocket, and wore a slouch hat. I found out he was the supervisor.

"Who sent you?"

"The big boss," I said. "Don't you know the big boss?"

I proceeded with the other masons, who had arrived by now, to the elevator. I went up with them and started to work. I figured I could work alongside the men for a while, then step back when I got tired, to supervise. But as soon as I exerted myself the nausea began. So I stepped back and waited for it to pass. Same thing happened again. This went on for about two hours.

Now the foreman came and told me, nervously, to go down to the shed, there was someone who wanted to talk to me. I told myself I had nothing to fear, and down I went.

Here was a man all dressed up, with a suit, a necktie, and a slouch hat. He was no gentleman, though—a little rough-looking. Maybe he was the chief contractor or the union representative for the job. I don't know, since he never identified himself, but he was clearly in charge. He just asked me, real cold and angry, "Who sent you?"

"The big boss," I said.

Well, he was furious. "I'm the big boss!" he screamed.

"Oh no you're not," I told him. "The big boss that sent me is bigger than you."

He couldn't believe it for a second, and then he said, "You mean the secretary?" I knew he meant the union secretary.

"You see," I said, "Now you know the big boss."

And he told the foreman that it was okay for me to work. Now I had a job, and they couldn't deny me my union card.

By this time I was beginning to realize that the nausea wasn't going away. I was in the shed with the other masons at lunchtime, unable to eat, when the shop steward angrily called me out and led me to the phone.

The steward directed me to dial the secretary's number. As soon as I identified myself to the secretary, he started yelling at the top of his lungs, threatening me. I waited for him to finish.

Sick as I was, I could only think, I didn't come this far to get thrown off the job. He wasn't bothering to lower his voice, so I didn't bother to lower mine. "Listen, creep," I told him. "I'm playing by the rules of Taft-Hartley. You and your cronies want to use any angle to stop legitimate people like me from working. I swear—if you come to this job and try to stop me, no one would prevent me from throwing you off the roof. I'm following your rules, I just got hired to a union job, and I demand a union card!"

"What are you," he said, "Some kind of lawyer?"

"No," I said. But I knew the fine print on the Taft-Hartley Law, and I told him the important parts. He coughed on the other end of the line. Then he blew his nose or something.

He told me to go ahead, but he was going to look it up for himself. "I know where to find you," he said, and then hung up.

And that was it. I could stay on the job; I could get my card. All this to get a job. It was crazy.

I only made it through another two hours that day before I knew I was going to vomit blood again. I left immediately and went back to the Veteran's Hospital.

The doctor gave me a new diagnosis: ulcers and depression. He told me, "You've got to find a new line of work."

***

So it was back to Arthur Avenue and Fordham Road. Things had changed here since the Depression ended. Fordham

University had grown. So had everything else, including the hospital, the small offices, and businesses. When I went to the diner at the corner for a cup of coffee, I saw a lot of young professionals now—doctors and lawyers. On Fordham Road there were a travel agency, an insurance agency, and a real estate broker. The realtor was a little Italian-American man, bald and dark, whom the guys seemed to know pretty well. I heard from them that he'd been there a long time. His family was from the neighborhood, and was pretty well off. He had a twin brother who was a doctor.

One of the guys from the old days had even become a lawyer. He came up to me as I was sitting at the counter in the diner one day.

"Armand," he said from behind me.

What a complete shock. I turned around and knew him right away, even though I hadn't seen him in years. He was in a suit, over six feet tall, and yet he looked just the same. "Gene! Gene Crescenzi!" I yelled.

"How are you, Armand?"

It was great to see him again. Gene had always been one of the brightest boys in school. We'd been good friends, although his father was not in manual labor like mine. His family had a little money, even during the Depression.

"What have you been doing, Gene?" I said. "I haven't seen you since high school."

Gene laughed. "What else, I got drafted! I did my time in Japan, but I got out before Korea started. I went to school. The Army paid part of the tuition. Armand, they paid for me to go to law school."

"A Veteran's benefit?"

"Well, only $110 a month. My family took care of the rest. And now I take care of them."

I nodded. That's how it should be.

I mentioned Gene to my father at breakfast the next day.

"*Gazz'*," he said. "Big shot, eh? *U'professor'.*" And he went back to drinking his coffee. A young man spending money and wasting time to read books at a desk? He didn't believe in it.

Forget it, I thought. College was not for me; I'd never make it without help. But I started thinking about how I might be able to make a living using my brains. In the meantime my veteran's benefit was a $26-a-week unemployment allowance, and it wouldn't last long, only 26 weeks from the time I was discharged. I was halfway through it.

What did I have to lose? I made up my mind to visit the realtor on Fordham Road and ask about getting a job. I had a suit in the closet from my contracting days. In the morning, I put it on.

The suit reminded me of the first time that I ever wore a suit, borrowed from a friend for my high school graduation. My mother was so proud when I graduated, the only one from my family, and I'm talking about the first ever, for as long as anyone could remember. Our people in Italy were peasants.

My father had been proud, too, but he couldn't tell me that. It wasn't his way. Instead, when I stepped out of the bedroom on graduation morning, while my mother held me at arm's length and admired me, Pop had said, "Ah! Now you're a big shot. Don't act like a bum."

He always used to call white-collar workers bums. He said they made their living off the honest men who worked with their backs, like he did.

My mother had just said, as she bustled us out the door, "Aah! My son is a gentleman!"

Wearing a suit might not really make a gentleman, but I was determined to prove that I was no bum, even though I couldn't work like my father and brothers.

The broker looked up as I stepped into Fordham Road Realty.

"Yeah, how can I help you?" he said. He looked me up and down, recognizing me from the street, suspicious about me losing my blue-collar clothes.

"The name's Miele, Armand Miele," I said. "I hope you don't mind, but I'm interested in the real estate business. I see you're all alone here. I was wondering if you could use a salesman."

He let out a short laugh. "Alone is right," he said. "Well, what's your background?"

"I was a contractor before the Korean War," I began.

"Veteran, huh? What'd you say your name was?"

"Miele, Armand Miele."

He snapped his fingers. "You're the guy who did the work for the Grand company a couple of years ago! Carpenter?"

"Cement," I said. From then on, he was easy to talk to. I knew a little about real estate from my contracting days. I had poured cement for various owners and landlords, including the acquaintances this broker mentioned. I told him this, and said, by way of showing my honest interest, "Real estate seems like a nice living."

He gave another of those short laughs. "It's not bad," he said, "Not bad. But listen, your first step is to get your license. Then come back and we'll get you to work." He sent me to the Department of State to get the study materials for the licensing test.

Starting the next day, I visited the Fordham broker daily. He seemed bored by himself, and enjoyed teaching me the business, so we became friendly. We looked at different houses, and he told me this and that about which houses sell for how much, and why. I began to feel comfortable with the idea of earning a living this way.

My mother tried so hard to help. She assured me that this was good experience, and gave me, I swear, 25 cents—all that she could afford—whenever she could. I felt bad about it. But she didn't want me to give up just because I couldn't make my own money right away, and I saw the sense in that.

I worked hard studying—state laws about land use, about what you must tell a prospect before you allow a contract to be signed, about informing the customer of defects. All that. I had no problem with the licensing test.

License in hand, I went to work for my friend, the Fordham broker, the first gentleman I'd known personally. I gave him all my respect; I kept my mouth shut and listened. I wanted to learn as much as possible.

My first day in the office, I got the lowdown. "You'll make money on sales commissions only," he said. No surprise there. I knew that this was the norm in the real estate business. "Now the rules of the store. Rule one: You do not have a key to the office. I don't want you to think I mistrust you, but this is my place and I want to be the one to open up and lock up. Period. Rule two: I am not here to feed you. You pay your own way, for a cup of coffee, for a sandwich, whatever. Rule three: You don't talk to my clients. That just makes things simpler. You know which clients are yours, I know which are mine, and we know who gets paid for what. That's all."

I thought the rules a little odd. Was he afraid I would take advantage of him? Steal his sales? But I resolved not to question him. Maybe that's just how office work was. Who knew, this was a whole new world for me. We went to the diner down the street, where the Fordham broker usually got a mid-morning cup of coffee. I didn't order anything, with the excuse that I didn't drink coffee. I couldn't let him know I was broke.

This was the summer of 1952. My last Veteran's check came. I bought an extra white shirt and a couple of ties. My mother washed my shirts, getting them as white as she did when I was six years old and just starting school. They were whiter than the Fordham broker's, for sure. My brother Augie helped me find a car, a used Buick Special, which we bought for $25 and an old football uniform I'd picked up back in high school.

I spent the next eight months taking customers out to look at houses and using up my mother's quarters for gas money. I ate my coffee and bread in the morning with my family, worked all day seven days a week, and came home at dark for dinner, just as I did when I was a child, except that I'd made more money shining shoes and plucking chickens.

I didn't make a single sale. I couldn't understand why it should be so difficult. When I showed people homes I was very polite. I drove them in my own car. It seemed like I was always out, showing houses, but when I checked in with the Fordham broker, there were never any messages from customers. I wondered why no one ever called me back. The Fordham broker, though, seemed to be making a good living. In the eight months I spent in that office, making nothing, he took loads of phone calls, all, apparently, for him. He made two or three good deals. He had plenty of money to eat out every day.

I worked through the winter, driving my car out to Yonkers and all over the Bronx, no matter the weather. Spring came and passed. I'd been to see so many properties that I knew this part of New York like the back of my hand. Still not one sale. What was I doing wrong?

It was completely by chance that I ran into one of these customers on the street one day, a man who had been looking to buy a multi-family home, something that would allow him to live in one apartment and rent out the rest. I had shown his wife a three-family apartment house in the Bronx. He told me he'd called the office to ask for me. The boss had said I wasn't in.

"Oh yeah?" I said. "That's funny. I didn't get the message."

And that might have been that, except that after I saw him I happened to walk by a newsstand, and there was the New York Times, the edition with the real estate section, right on the counter. Maybe the guy had given me a funny feeling. Anyway, I bought the paper. They carried announcements of all the houses that sold. Sure enough, there was the house I showed to the man's wife.

I was so crushed. I'd missed a sale, missed paying back my mother's quarters, missed sitting down with the Fordham broker for some lunch and a cup of coffee! If only I had gotten that phone call!

I went straight to the Fordham broker. I knew it would be hard to prove, but maybe we could sue whoever sold the property I had shown those people. Maybe we could get them to pay us the commission we lost.

"Look here," I said as I hurried into the office. I held out the paper. "I showed those people this house, we've got to sue them, we got no commission."

The Fordham broker looked at me. "You didn't show it," he said.

"What do you mean? Sure I did. I worked to get them there. I brought them back and forth."

He shook his head. "No."

And it dawned on me. This guy had stolen my sale. He'd been doing it all along; that's why he would tell me, "Don't answer the phone." I never really had a chance to make a deal. Eight months of my life.

"You're a crook," I told him, right to his face. "You're a dirty bastard."

There was no fight, no argument. I didn't even say that I was quitting. I just walked out. This was the man my father warned me about, years ago at high school graduation. This bum, this heartless phony, this crook in a suit.

The next morning I went to see Gene Crescenzi. His office was in a three-story building, just like the one I should have sold. He had his office on the second floor, and he lived with his parents on the top. The first floor was vacant.

"Armand!" he said, happy to see me. "What's up?"

I told him the story of the Fordham broker. I knew it probably wasn't worth it, but I was angry, and I asked Gene whether I could sue for my commission.

Gene was smiling at me when I finished, but he shook his head. "Naw, Armand, you'll never get him," he said. "What are you going to use as proof against him? That he answered the phone in his own office? Forget it. You're better off going somewhere else."

"But Gene, he's a dirty bastard."

"Armand, you bide your time. You stay in the business, and don't back down. You'll get him one day. Or even better, you'll do better than him. People know he's a creep, they'll come to you because you are a gentleman."

That was my mother's word, "gentleman." Gene's words encouraged me, but I was disappointed that I wouldn't get my commission. Back to square one again.

Gene invited me up to see his parents. He'd told them he ran into me, he said, and they'd love to see me.

We knocked on the door of the upstairs apartment, and it was as if Mrs. Crescenzi was expecting us. The table was set with dishes, cups, coffee and cake.

"Ma," Gene said, "Here's Armand!"

You'd have thought I was a long-lost relative. "Armand!" she said, all excited, "Gene told us he saw you! God bless you! How are you? Gene says you were such good friends as boys. Come in, come on, have some coffee!"

I protested only a little. The coffee smelled as good as my mother's, the strong Italian coffee that you couldn't get in a diner. In my family, we didn't eat cake even on birthdays, unless Frankie brought it. Mr. Crescenzi, another big guy, came in from somewhere with dirt on his shoes. He took them off before coming to the table. He was just as happy to see me as his wife and son.

"Armand!" he said, admiring my suit. "Here's another kid from the neighborhood all grown up, huh?" He slapped me on the back, and we sat down to coffee.

"Real estate, huh?" Mr. Crescenzi said, when I'd told him a little about my doings. "Be careful. You can't be too good to people."

"Mr. Crescenzi, I know it. I found out the hard way."

"Well, better now than never," he said. "You're young. Real estate can make you a good living. We have a building down Manhattan, an apartment building, it carried us through the Depression."

I saw Mrs. Crescenzi and Gene both shaking their heads, and Gene said, "A nice building. What were there in the beginning, Pop, three or four apartment buildings?"

"Four," Mr. Crescenzi said, "But I had to sell three."

He stopped, and Gene picked up the story. "The people weren't paying the rent. He was too good to them! The Depression--he figured, go easy on them, they can't pay it. Well, it turns out, one was gambling with his rent money, one was buying booze. They were just using the money for other things."

"What? The rent's gotta come first!" I said.

"Ah," said Mr. Crescenzi, "You know it, because your father knew it, and that's how he kept a roof over his family." It was true. My father was still always worrying about the rent, turning off all the lights, and arguing with my mother in the dark.

We talked about our families then. Mrs. Crescenzi showed a picture of all her sons together, Gene and his two brothers, all big like their father. One, she said, was in the CIA. The other was a doctor. All of them were educated and well-off, given a good start by the rent income from one building.

Mr. Crescenzi invited me to see his garden, while Mrs. Crescenzi cleaned up. "Armand, you gotta see this," Gene said.

We went out in the hall, but instead of heading down the stairs, Mr. Crescenzi went up a little ladder leading to the roof. We followed him up through a trap door. I figured we'd be able to see the garden from the roof. I pictured a plot in a vacant lot, like my father's farm from my childhood, only smaller. But instead of climbing out onto tar and shingles, my hands felt dirt. I put my head through the trapdoor in the roof and stood there gaping for so long that Gene had to give me a shove from behind before I remembered to climb all the way out.

"You've got to be kidding," I yelled. I laughed. "This is unbelievable!"

There were lettuces, herbs, eggplants, peppers, string beans, each in their own little box of eight-inch wide planks, in good, deep beds of black dirt. The all-important tomatoes had almost half the roof to themselves, strong vines climbing up through cages made of found wood of all thicknesses and lengths. There were flowers. A tree in a pot.

"*Madonn'*," I said. Gene and his father were laughing at me. "How did you do it?"

"You can get the dirt at the zoo. They'll let you have it with all the fertilizer mixed in from the animals," Mr. Crescenzi told me.

"But all this dirt!" I said. "It must have taken you a year!"

He shook his head and made a dismissive sound, but Gene said, "At least."

Mr. Crescenzi was so proud of that garden. He took me around, showing me every plant. We sat in little chairs near the tree, a very young cherry tree (it was too little to sit "under"), and had a cigarette. We talked until the sun started to go down.

The smell of dinner began to come up from Mrs. Crescenzi's kitchen window. I got up to leave.

"Armand, stay!" Mr. Crescenzi urged, but I told them I should get home. My mother was making dinner for me, too. I knew she looked forward to seeing me at the end of the day.

Gene said, "Armand, come back tomorrow. I have to talk to you about something."

"Yeah?" I said. "All right, Gene, I'll see you tomorrow."

I left them sitting in the garden. I stopped in on Mrs. Crescenzi to say goodbye, and refused politely when she urged me to stay. Her kitchen smelled as good as my own mother's.

When I got home, the pasta was almost ready. My mother had seen me coming home and thrown it in the pot, just as she used to do for my father.

At the table, I told Catherine and my parents about Gene Crescenzi. My mother was thrilled, but she told me, sort of as a warning, I guess, "Armand, *sta'ci con tu'miglio', ma paghi tu'via.*" Go with your betters, but pay your own way. It was her way of reminding me not to shame myself, or the family, by taking charity.

I told my father about Mr. Crescenzi's tomato plants, and about my amazement at the roof garden. He grunted, nodded, and drank his wine without saying anything. His farm, where all us boys had worked as children, was long gone. As we'd gotten older and gone to work—one for a grocer, one for a butcher—we didn't need what he grew anymore. We also didn't have time to help him tend things, and of course he couldn't do it himself, because he was working too. It had gone back to being a vacant lot after awhile, and then someone built something on it.

After dinner, Pop got up to take his walk. My mother and Catherine cleaned up while I read the newspaper. I wondered what my mother and father talked about when I wasn't at home.

Then Pop came home and turned off all the lights. I heard my mother sigh, "*La luce, la luce!*" as she always did when she wasn't ready for the lights to go out.

My father grumbled, "*La luce cost'i soldi,*" and they said no more about it.

The next day I visited Gene early, and found him in his office. He had a proposal for me. It wasn't great for the value of his building, he said, for the first floor apartment to remain empty, but he couldn't get a good tenant.

"Why don't you make it an office?" he said. "I'm an attorney, and I can act as your broker. And since it's still technically my office, you don't need to pay rent."

The offer was a godsend. Like God led me right there and handed me a living and a good friend all at once. A fantastic friend. I took him up on it on the spot, and got back to work that very day.

I finally started to make a few sales. Gene had to close the deals, because he was the broker, but he never took his cut of the commission. I tried to pay him back in different ways, picking up the tab when we went for lunch or a drink, but I knew I could never really repay him. I never gave a backward thought to the Fordham broker; in fact I never spoke his name again. Gene was right. My business was to make my profession a priority, and to succeed as a gentleman. Also, if anything, the Fordham broker had done me a favor, because otherwise how would I have ended up with Gene? Gene's mother still tried to feed me every day; his father was always praising me.

Even so, it wasn't easy. With perseverance alone I got by. I was too honest to ever become a really good salesman. There were actually times when I worried for the clients. Some of them really had too little money to maintain a home, and I tried not to sell to them. When I did sell, I never tried to take advantage of a client's ignorance by taking extra fees or inflating the commission, as I had seen others do. I had the foresight to see when there were other deals to be made, deals worth good money, but in real estate, when you have little money yourself, there is only so much you can do. Often I could do nothing. The deals were too few and far between for me to catch up easily.

Then, in 1955, three things happened almost at the same time.

First, I was able to rack up enough experience in the business that I could get my broker's license. Second, a real estate office suddenly came up for sale in the neighborhood. The owner, who was about 65, wanted to retire. He offered his office to me, a busy, corner location on Esplanade Avenue. It was a tremendous opportunity, but also a tremendous responsibility. Would I be able to make it? I took the chance, and was able to pay him off after only a few sales. Now, I thought, the worries will begin.

Third, at my sister Catherine's wedding, I found out that my mother was very sick. Catherine waited until after the reception to tell me about it.

"She came with me when I got my blood test last month," Catherine said. It was the law in those days that everyone had to get a blood test 30 days before they got married. "She says to the doctor, 'Doctor, could you please tell me what you think of this,' and she shows him her breast. Armand, she has a lump like a pound of butter right here." Catherine showed me with her hands an area the shape of a rectangle just above and to the left of her heart.

"What?" I was ready to hunt down the doctor and kill him. "Why didn't he take it out?"

"Armand, he wanted to, but she wouldn't let him until after the wedding!" Catherine was crying now. "He said if it had been there long enough to get this big, he guessed that thirty days wouldn't make much difference. Armand, do you think he was wrong? Did I do wrong, letting her wait?"

"All right, Catherine, all right," I said, quieting my voice. She'd just gotten married, after all, and should be able to celebrate her own wedding. "If the doctor said it was fine, of course you didn't do wrong. Don't worry, I'll be here. I'll be here. All right?"

She didn't really cheer up, but she stopped crying. Inside, I was furious at the doctor. But I could also imagine how my mother must have protested the operation. "Don't touch me! After my daughter's wedding I'll stay in the hospital forever. But until then, *non mi toccare!*"

***

I brought my mother to the hospital for the first time on Sunday, June 26th, the day Catherine went away for her honeymoon. It was difficult for me to leave my new office closed for the day. On these springtime Sundays, Esplanade Avenue in the afternoon would take on a holiday feeling, with all the people dressed nicely, relaxing, and spending time together. The married couples would take their afternoon walks, and some of those couples would stop in my office. Of those, many would be like window shoppers, just coming in to get information, not really ready to own a home. It gave me the opportunity to introduce myself. One day they might come back. And even one serious couple could mean a sale. I hated to imagine the Sunday crowd reading the little sign on my door that read, "Open 7 days, 9am-6pm," and finding me closed.

Early in the morning, I helped my mother into the car. Not knowing whether the lump in her breast was painful, I was as careful as I could be. "Ma," I said as she settled herself, "You all right?"

"Sure, I'm all right," she said. "Let's go." She was wearing the same sort of Sunday clothes as the window shoppers would wear later. Her white handbag matched her shoes. She smiled at me. I closed the door and got into the driver's seat.

I don't know who found Dr. Virgilio Ciampa, the surgeon, for my mother. Maybe he was just assigned to her that day because he happened to speak Italian. I knew him very slightly from the diner on Fordham Road. All the doctors would stop in there for a cup of coffee. When Dr. Ciampa met Ma in the examining room that day and said, *"Buon giorno, signora,"* she gave him a bigger smile than she had given the priest who married Catherine the day before. He asked her about herself in Italian, and she answered with more words than I'd heard her speak in months.

After the examination, he took me out to the hall to talk. He spoke to me in heavily accented English, but it wasn't broken, like my parents'. In fact, it was probably better than mine. He was a little shorter than me, maybe a little older too, and dark, like a Sicilian or a Calabrese. He offered me his hand, which I shook. He said, "Your mother's tumor is very large. That, we will deal with tomorrow. Today is just for tests, for her to settle in her room, for her to rest. But a lot of tests, we have to do."

"All right, Doctor," I said, wondering what he was getting at.

"Listen. You go, come back later. Believe me, you will do nothing here for her. It will be several hours. Do you have a phone number?"

I hesitated, then gave him my office number.

"Good," he said, patting me on the shoulder. "I'll call you, if anything. Meantime give it until maybe six tonight, by the time she gets settled. Then if you want, you come back and see what's what."

We went back into the room, and he explained to my mother that he was sending me away. But she already trusted Dr. Ciampa so much that she didn't mind. "Go on," she said to me. "I'm all right. *Mi vieni a dopo.*" Come back to me later.

***

I spent the rest of the day at my new office, talking to the window shoppers. It was like starting over with every customer that walked through the door. When I made a sale, that money would pay the bills and leave very little left over.

The office was in a beautiful location, which made up for it being sort of plain. I had the desks that the last broker left me, one for myself, and two others for the associates I planned to have one day. I only had one phone. There was no such thing as an answering machine, of course. I was careful to make only important calls, and I didn't stay long on the phone, for fear of running up a large bill.

I felt that you couldn't sell property if you didn't look successful, so I dressed well. My wardrobe consisted of only short-sleeved wash-and-wear shirts, black socks, one sport jacket, and two suits. I owned a lot of ties, so I didn't feel that I looked the same every day. I had one pair of brown shoes, one black, always shined. I had a raincoat. That was it. I took care of my clothes.

I spent only when I had no other choice. I knew exactly what I had in my pocket, down to the penny, and every time I had to pay a bill it was like giving blood.

Would I leave this office an old man, like the man I bought it from? I couldn't imagine spending my life there. I told myself that this would be temporary. Once I made a really good deal, I'd be an owner-landlord, not just a broker.

Many of the couples I encountered were new immigrants. They were often able to buy a home after only a few years in this country, even though their only income was from menial jobs: dishwashing, porting luggage, laboring in construction. When they came to me to buy a home, they made a huge down payment, sometimes all in cash. Meanwhile, the Americans who had been born here and were working the same jobs just couldn't make it. The immigrants had different priorities. The Americans spent beyond their means, going by what they thought they deserved, instead of what they could afford; the immigrants were thrifty. They didn't go into debt as long as they had the basics of food, shelter, and clothing.

The immigrants were not from cities. They were from the small villages of their countries. Those in the large cities, who were doing well, didn't leave their countries, for the most part. The villagers looked to escape hunger and poverty, and America gave them opportunities they couldn't find in their homelands. Italy, for instance, was still recovering from World War II. For most Italian villagers, there was just no work to be had.

American families gave up the cheap, unimproved top-floor walk-ups in the poor neighborhoods. The immigrants were happy to take them. The luxuries of heat, hot and cold running water, a toilet that flushed, and electricity just didn't exist in the Italian countryside at that time. On top of the improved living quarters, people could walk to the local store. The new immigrants bought all kinds of food and comforts that they could never have before. Even the cheapest cuts of meat and the oldest vegetables were often better than what they could get at home.

Some of them said to themselves, "America is great, but I will go home once I've saved enough. I will go home a rich man." They wanted to share their good fortune with the family back home, and live like kings. But then they got to know the American lifestyle, and things started to change.

It would begin this way. In a family new to this country, everyone worked and pooled their earnings, even the children. It was not a sacrifice to save money. They felt that they had everything they needed and more, at least at first. Every week they deposited money in the bank, which gained interest. In the village, of course, there had been no banks.

The problems would start when they bought their first car, then a television. They'd decide they wanted to move to a still better neighborhood, and then of course they'd need new furniture. Guess what? They became Americano. Welcome to the mainstream! They couldn't go back. Once the farmer sees Rome, is he going back to the farm? No way. You pay for a lifestyle one way or another. This is nothing to complain about, but just how I saw it go with a lot of the immigrant families.

Professional men like Virgilio Ciampa, who emigrated from Italy only in the last five years, had different problems. When I went back to the hospital that evening, he was waiting for me in my mother's room with a typical immigrant's problem: income taxes. Ma looked a little anxious, worrying about the surgery I thought, so I figured Dr. Ciampa was there to make her comfortable with his kind and respectful conversation. But as soon as Ma laid eyes on me, she said, "Armand! There you are. Look, Dr. Ciampa needs help with his taxes. *Parli con lui*."

I'd been doing my father's taxes since I was 12, and of course I'd been doing my own taxes too, ever since I went into business before the Korean War. After settling my mother for the night, Dr. Ciampa joined me for a cup of coffee at the Fordham Road diner.

As we sat down for coffee, he told me that the tumor was even larger than he'd expected. The surgery was likely to take more than a couple of hours tomorrow, and he wasn't sure how she'd do afterward. "Sometimes these tumors, they come back," he said sadly. "Only time will tell. Meanwhile, we take good care of her, and we wait. And Armand–"

"Yes?"

"Just take good care of her. Keep her happy. That's the best medicine."

The talk turned to taxes. He had a letter from the IRS that he didn't understand. I read it and told him he owed some money in taxes.

"That's all?" he said.

It wasn't that he didn't have the money to pay; he'd just seen the official letterhead and gotten scared. I translated the letter for him, as well as I could in my parents' Italian dialect.

The change that came over him was amazing. He began to speak more loudly, more like the Italians I was used to from Arthur Avenue. He called me a "wonder man"—maybe this was his Italian way of saying "Superman". "My God, Armand, do you know how worried I was about this?" he exclaimed. "But I should pay you. You should charge me a fee."

I was taken aback. "No!" I said. "What are you, kidding? You're saving lives in my neighborhood. You're saving my mother's life! And you're going to pay me! No way."

"Armand, please!" he insisted. "You can't imagine all the problems you've saved me."

"Dr. Ciampa, stop it."

"Call me Virgilio."

"All right, Virgilio. Stop it! It's an honor to help you. Don't you dare mention it again." I reached into my pocket to pay for the coffee. If I hadn't known I could pay for both of us, I wouldn't have invited him for coffee in the first place. I put a single on the counter and took him back to the hospital. He asked whether I could look at some letters and forms for friends of his who didn't read English well. Of course I agreed.

My mother's surgery was extensive, as Virgilio had explained, but it went well. He didn't think he'd need to operate again. For the two weeks that she recovered in the hospital, I was a frequent visitor. Catherine, too, when she returned from her trip, kept Ma company while her husband, Bill, was at work.

Virgilio and I frequently went for lunch or a cup of coffee after that, often with a doctor who needed a letter translated or a form filled out. Sometimes, when I saw how relieved some of these men would be over the resolution of something simple, and heard their expressions of gratitude, I realized they really had no one else to turn to. It made me think of Gene Crescenzi helping me out. I had never managed to pay him back; I didn't want to be paid back, either. I felt I was being repaid plenty, in the respect and friendship that these educated, honorable gentlemen offered to me. I never had friends like these, friends I could have a conversation with.

I still saw the Crescenzis quite a bit. They had sort of adopted me since Ma had been in the hospital. I'd sometimes see Augie or Jimmy with their families on a Sunday. If Frank happened to be there too, it was almost like old times. But I'd usually feel like a fifth wheel, with the wives all fussing about the children, and my brothers absorbed in family life, unable to relax. Catherine liked to cook for me sometimes, but she was newly married, which made me feel in the way. When I was with her and Bill I was always wondering when I should leave. It was the Crescenzis' table I came to again and again, where Mr. and Mrs. Crescenzi and my friend Gene took great interest in my doings, and I in theirs.

Ma went home after a couple of weeks. Catherine did everything she could for her, but Pop seemed to talk even less. I hated to be around at dinnertime. Cooking and housework seemed harder for Ma now, and I felt I should take care of myself now that I was beginning to make a better living.

Over the next couple of years, I followed my mother's advice, to go with my betters, but pay my own way. One thing I must say is that I was never cheap. I didn't want that reputation. I never went to a restaurant with friends unless I knew I could pick up the entire check. Don't get me wrong; my friends treated me many times. I was respected throughout Pelham Parkway, the best neighborhood in the Bronx, and I was meeting wonderful new people. I may have been broke at times, but no one had to know that. Certainly not these Italian doctors, who still thought I could take care of anything, just because I knew how to file income taxes.

These young doctors never had a full night's sleep, or much time for anything but work, but they kept up their spirits by laughing a lot. There were so many fun stories.

Virgilio came to me one day. "Armand," he said to me in Italian, "You taught me to order in English a ham sandwich. It's all I know how to order, 'Ham sand-u-wich, coffee.' I'm tired of it!"

So I taught him to say "ham and cheese."

The next time I saw him, he told me that "ham and cheese" was no good.

"Why, Virgilio," I said, "I thought you wanted something different."

"It's no good," he insisted in Italian. "I ordered 'ham and cheese,' just like you said, and the waitress gave me trouble. She tried to make me order something else. I said again, 'ham and cheese, coffee.' She wouldn't get it for me. I thought maybe it was my accent, so I tried one more time. Still she gave me trouble."

Turned out that the waitress was asking him, "American, Swiss, or Cheddar?" The poor guy didn't understand a word she said, so he went back to "Ham sand-u-wich, coffee."

Cesare Cucci, another of the Italian doctors who I got to know, was working in the emergency room when a couple came in arguing. The husband took Cesare aside. "Doctor," he said, "Please don't tell my wife that I have the clap."

Dr. Cucci had been educated in England; he prided himself on his excellent English. He wasn't familiar with the American slang term "the clap," but he understood that the man needed him to keep whatever it was a secret. After the examination, when the man's wife came to ask what was wrong with her husband, Cesare explained to her, "Your husband has a perfectly curable disease. It's just a simple case of gonorrhea."

He didn't mention the clap, so he couldn't understand why his remark unleashed such pandemonium.

I even got in on the act once. I was visiting the hospital with another guy from the neighborhood, a sharp dresser; we used to call him "Snazzy Joe". We were on the elevator, both of us looking good, well-dressed and professional. The elevator was very quiet, and I guess he felt like we needed to have a laugh. He started talking to me in a very serious, low voice, putting on that we were doctors, and he was telling me about a grave case. Only he was whispering total nonsense to me, trying to make me crack up. Nobody on the elevator made a sound. If somebody thinks you're a doctor, you get that extra respect.

Everyone in the elevator was hanging on every word, even though only every other one made sense, pretending not to look at us, barely breathing. It was completely silent except for Joe's gibberish.

I finally nodded my head and said, "Doctor, you're a genius. We'll have to write it up."

And just when neither of us thought we could hold it in anymore, the elevator doors opened, and we stepped out with everybody staring after us, speechless, from being so close to the presence of genius, I guess. We busted out laughing before the doors closed behind us.

This was 1957. We were visiting Ma, who was back in the hospital. It had taken a couple of years, but the cancer had returned.

Joe and I were still chuckling as we entered her room, which was just how she liked to see visitors: with a joke to tell or a story from the neighborhood, not with the same hangdog expression she used to make fun of on my father's face.

Above Top: My mother and me in the weeks before she died.

Above: Amaroni, Italy

Above Left: My friend Virgilio Ciampa and his bride

Left: My bride and me, with her maid of honor and my best man, Gilda and Cesare Cucci

Ofelia

A Love So Far Above Me

By 1959, I began to feel like I was going to make it financially, but the first taste of success was bittersweet. I had always been driven by the desire to help the family, to give something back to my parents. Now that I was in the position to give back, I found out that providing for my parents was really beyond my power. Ma's health was not improving. Pop, who had always been the provider, always in charge, was too proud to guide me in how to help. Instead, I had to guess at ways to keep them comfortable and happy.

Old age could be so uncomfortable and uncertain. Look at Mr. Ernesto Manzi, a sales agent who'd begun as my associate around 1958. The way his life had gone taught me something.

Nice man, Mr. Manzi: clean, honest, and well-spoken, like a real gentleman. But money was a problem for him. That's all he talked about, money, money, money. Here he was, 65 years old, more than double my age, and yet he needed to count to the penny how much he had in his pocket. Mr. Manzi was a retired accountant. He'd been living well on his Social Security, when his wife passed away and he remarried. The new wife changed everything. He had to dress nicely and drive a new car. These things were important to her. And there were other things she wanted: a vacation to Florida, her own new car, and weekly visits to the hairdresser. But he'd never told her that he didn't have that kind of money. Her spending cleaned him out. He went broke, and had to go back to work.

I swore that would never happen to me.

The day I saw the first big deal I would make, the one that would put me in business for real, I was at the office looking over a life insurance policy that would pay $10,000 in 30 years. In walked Mr. Manzi.

"Any messages for me?" he said.

"Yep, a Mr. Greco. Number's on your desk. Get in there, Mr. Manzi."

Mr. Manzi had been relieved to get work as a salesman with me. He and I both knew how the business worked in most real estate offices. Sales agents had to play the Fordham broker's game. You had to watch your back or get killed. And they'd do anything to sell, not caring what the customer could afford or who they screwed. Sell, sell, sell! I just didn't believe in that.

Mr. Manzi was on the phone when another call came in, so I took it. It was a client I'd done business with a few times, a landlord, interested in selling a single-family house with an apartment. I told him I'd be over later in the morning. Meanwhile Mr. Manzi, still on the phone, was trying to get my attention. He put his hand over the receiver and asked me, "Armand, okay if I take an appointment this afternoon?"

"Sure," I said, "I can be here later."

He signed off with Mr. Greco, and started tearing through the cards we filed for all the listings, copying information into his little notebook. He counted the money from his pocket, making sure he could buy Mr. Greco a cup of coffee later, if he had to. It was great to have an associate so on the ball, but still, seeing this older man driven back to work by a messy second marriage made me start to think about my own security. There was no doubt in my mind that the same thing could happen to me, if I didn't plan ahead. When your family needs money, if there's any way you can provide it, how can you say no?

On my way to visit my client's property, I planned to check on the new apartment. I'd taken the apartment in Yonkers with my mother a year ago, when her frequent trips to the hospital, traveling to and from the Bronx, began to make her life even more uncomfortable and exhausting. She was in the hospital right now. After checking on the apartment, I'd go relieve Catherine at the hospital. She needed to go home and make dinner for her family, and had been sitting with Ma all afternoon.

I arrived on time to meet my client. He was an elderly man who wanted to free up some of his money, to be able to enjoy his retirement. It was a nice house, on two lots. I agreed to list it for $19,000.

***

It had been a bad time for Ma, after the cancer came back in 1957. Virgilio had operated again, to remove another tumor. He'd also removed Ma's pituitary gland, hoping to stop the cancer from coming back a third time. To do that surgery they needed to cut off all her hair. It never grew back right, and became very thin and grey.

She had come home after a couple of weeks with terrible pain and swelling in her legs. I had to give her injections for the pain. I felt awful, sticking her with the big needles. You used the same needle, day after day, just cleaning it with a little alcohol and warming it for each shot. Sometimes the woman who lived upstairs would come by to visit, to see if there was anything she could do, and she would look at me with pity. I don't know why. I wasn't the one who was sick.

Of course, Ma couldn't cook the hot meals that my father expected every night. She could barely lift the pasta bat. Housework was out of the question. Even conversation was a big effort for her, especially with my father, because he didn't know how to comfort her. There had been only one way to deal with illness in his life. The survival and well-being of the family meant breaking his back every day, no matter what. If he got sick, he worked through it.

Things got easier between them after I got her the Yonkers apartment, though. It was a place where she could rest, and my brothers, sister, and I could take care of her. Every Sunday we had the family meal there, cooked now by my sister and my brothers' wives. But the weeks alone were long and painful for her.

The Yonkers apartment had everything Ma had always wanted: a doorman, an elevator, a neighborhood with gardens and more space between the buildings, not like our old tenement. It was a real comfortable place, with lots of light coming through windows that let in the breeze in the summer, and shut out the drafts in the winter. But Ma didn't know her neighbors, and was too sick and self-conscious to visit, so she kept to herself. When neighbors did come to say hello, they treated her like a sick old woman, which she hated. I still gave her the injections every day and made sure she was comfortable. Between Catherine and my brothers' wives, she had visitors every day, but she never got her old spirit back.

As for my father, when Ma and I moved to the new Yonkers place, I think he grew lonely too. But he never spoke about it. I still visited him to reassure him about Ma's health and tell him everything that was going on. We all visited him, when we could, and of course he would get a ride with one of us to the family meal each Sunday in Yonkers. But he rarely visited Ma in the hospital, even though we could tell he missed her.

"*Non ti preoccupà*', Pop," I told him. "Don't worry. We're taking care of Ma. Just come when you can."

A younger woman from the neighborhood started coming around to cook and clean for him, so we knew he was taken care of. But it felt strange having her in my father's apartment. I never stayed for long when she was around. I would take my leave politely, hoping I was not hurting my father's feelings.

***

When I entered Ma's room later that day, Catherine was already there, looking ready to cry, but that wasn't unusual.

"You just missed Frankie," she said. "*Madonn'*, Armand, Ma's seeing things!"

I bent down to kiss my mother. She gave me a tired smile. I noticed she was getting very thin.

"Armand," she said, with the Italian inflection that no one else used.

"Take it easy, Catherine," I said. "Who'd you see, Ma?"

"What?" she said. "You here, and Catherine. They're not here to give me another shot, are they? It never ends!" Her voice was weak and rough. The medication was making speech difficult; she slurred her words.

"No, not yet, Ma," Catherine said.

Then Ma looked over toward the door. "*Chi è*, who is it, Stephen?" she said. Stephen was Catherine's oldest son. He was with a neighbor back in the Bronx. "Catherine, make Stephen come in. *Vieni qui, cecharell'!*"

"No, Ma, it's just Catherine and me," I said.

Catherine began to fall apart. "You see, Armand?" she said.

"I'm gonna get some sleep," Ma said, closing her eyes. "Catherine, get Stephen to come in. *Non si preoccupà. Non dev'avere paura*. He shouldn't be afraid."

So, Catherine wasn't overreacting. We were both heartbroken to leave our mother that afternoon, but she happily let us kiss and embrace good-bye. "*Ciao*," she said. "Don't worry. I feel good. *Mi vedet'a'dopo*." See you later.

Catherine went back to the Bronx. Augie had promised to visit later, and Jimmy tomorrow morning; Frankie would come too. We took shifts. We didn't want to leave Ma alone.

In the morning, back in the office, thinking about Ma, who couldn't enjoy the comforts of her old age, I watched Mr. Manzi rush off to meet another customer, without hope of rest, probably until he died. On my desk was the letter I'd opened the day before, offering me a life insurance policy worth $10,000. At least, it would be worth $10,000 if I died; or I'd be entitled to collect that much in 30 years. I wondered what $10,000 would be worth in 30 years. Even at the time, $10,000 wouldn't buy a house: look at my client's house, which I planned to list for $19,000.

This is when the thought hit me: I'm going to buy that house myself.

I thought it over, and I was pretty sure I could swing the deal. I could make the mortgage payments with rent from the house and apartment, if I could get the bank to give me the mortgage. I'd have to be resourceful; it would take all my heart and determination, but, yes, I thought, I can swing this deal.

I called up the client and made my offer.

It was only a day or two later when I was in the middle of applying for my mortgage, getting the contracts together, and arranging for all the inspections I needed, that Catherine called me from Yonkers. Frankie had dropped her off there in the morning to clean up the apartment a little, and I was supposed to pick her up. I'd forgotten.

"Armand, I've been here since ten this morning," she said. "It's almost three now. No one's been to the hospital since last night."

"Oh, for—I'm sorry, Catherine." I had an appointment at the bank. "I can't come right now. Let me take you later."

And I went about my business. I got approved for my mortgage; I proceeded to the various offices I needed to visit to get the other arrangements made. It wouldn't be long before I owned a house. I thought about getting Catherine out of her neighborhood. None of us wanted the children to grow up in the tenements. Already I was considering whether I'd be able to put away enough money from the rent to buy another house. I was a little worried about making the mortgage payments, what with my office expense and the rent on the Yonkers apartment. It would be a real grind. But I knew how to budget myself. I'd just have to manage.

Late in the afternoon, I arrived back in my office. There was a message from Augie; he said to call the Yonkers apartment.

Catherine answered, her voice rough. "Mama's gone," she said.

I couldn't speak. I could barely listen.

"Augie went up there today, you know he was supposed to be with her this afternoon. Armand, he took his cement truck to the hospital!" She gave a little laugh, then she coughed. "He went to the room and there was nobody there." Now she began to cry again. "He asked the nurse, 'What happened to my mother?' Armand, she died last night, and nobody called. Nobody said anything."

I went up to Yonkers. Augie, Jimmy, Frankie, and Catherine were there. Not Pop. No spouses, no nieces and nephews. Just us. Catherine was making coffee. Jimmy had remembered to bring the anisette. "There's my baby brother," Augie said, coming to embrace me. "Mama's gone."

"Augie, I'm thirty years old." My voice was a whisper, like I was choking. But I hadn't been crying, not with tears, like Catherine.

"Geez, that's right," he said. "I'm sorry."

He never called me "baby" again.

At the funeral parlor a few days later, who should approach me but my mother's old upstairs neighbor. "It's better this way," she said. "Now you can live your life."

I wanted to kill her. I wanted to ask her, did you lose your mother? Was it easy for you? I'd been at the hospital twice a day, every day. I went because I wanted to. My brothers and my sister did the same. Still, she had died alone.

I let the Yonkers apartment go, and rented a little place in the old neighborhood, not far from my father. I avoided going there when the woman who cleaned and cooked was around. I never stayed for meals. But I didn't want my father to think he was forgotten. Almost immediately after my mother died, my father began getting thinner. He said he was eating plenty, but looking back, I think the sadness of the last two years had finally starting eating him.

When I told Mrs. Crescenzi that my mother had passed away, she asked, "How old was she?"

"Quite old," I said. "Fifty-three."

"Fifty-three! So young!"

I was astonished. To me, having watched my parents struggle all my life, it seemed Ma lived a long time. I was sure my father, too, felt like an old man. Anyone who had worked in manual labor since childhood, as he had, would feel the same way.

I'd had a job once, in between concrete jobs after high school, where I worked moving packages on a belt system. I retrieved packages off the belt as they came, and transferred them to a cage on wheels. I worked four p.m. to one a.m. Mind you, I lived in the Bronx, and this job was in downtown

Manhattan. I had to leave our apartment at two p.m. to walk to the Third Avenue elevated train, and arrive at work on time. I left work at one a.m., waited for the train, and didn't get home until four in the morning. I would unwind for an hour and then go to sleep. I woke up around noon or one p.m. to get ready to catch the train the next day.

Can you imagine a teenaged boy living this kind of life? Well, I thought at the time, imagine people doing this work for 25 and 30 years. Never mind the fact that I was a very proud high school graduate, who was not allowed to use my gift from God, my brains. Suppose I'd had a family at that age? If I wanted them to eat, that's the work I might have been stuck in. Imagining 25 or 30 years of hard, unrewarding hours made 53 seem a long way off to me.

My own life was unfolding differently, at the moment. I owned property. I had a tax deduction; I had appreciation on my investment, something I'd never had before; and the mortgage was paid every month. For the first time I was paying my bills with almost no worry. I was a young man, and I was building equity.

***

Within a year after my mother's death, my father sickened with lung cancer and died. It wasn't at all the long, sad parting that we'd had with Ma. It was a shock, more than anything. I'd known of men and women who died soon after their spouses; I always thought they must have been so close that they couldn't live without each other. I never thought of my parents being that way. I guess any marriage is deeper than what you see on the surface. My poor father. Who knows what he felt and suffered, without telling anyone.

My days fell into a different pattern now, with both Ma and Pop gone. I boiled myself an egg in the morning, and I went out for coffee. I spent my daytime hours either at the office or attending meetings with buyers and sellers. Lunch was at a diner or a restaurant with Gene or Frankie, unless I had a date with another agent or a client. In the evening, I often ate with the Crescenzis. On my own, I knew how to fry a steak, but those were the lonely nights. On those nights I missed my family the most. I missed my mother's pasta, rolled out with her bat and cut in her kitchen, her gravy, simmered on the back of the stove all afternoon, and the laughs we used to have over dinner, before everyone moved away, before Ma got sick.

The loneliness was hard, so I didn't sit with it night after night. I spent many evenings with my friends, and often they introduced me to women. The perfume these women wore was sometimes so strong, and the makeup so heavy! I was afraid to even touch them. But they were company.

As my friends began to pair off with the girlfriends they would one day marry, they all became anxious to see me settled as well. I couldn't imagine spending my life with any of these women. There was one that I went steady with for a while, but we both knew that marriage was wrong for us. Although we got along, there was often a silence between us during conversation, not because we were comfortable with each other, but because we disagreed and didn't want to be rude about it.

Virgilio was the first to go. His dentist introduced him to an Italian-American girl, and without really knowing what he was doing he found himself giving her an engagement ring.

"How could it happen so fast?" I asked him. I imagined he was going to answer with some old Italian saying about love at first sight.

Instead, he said in English, "Armand, God only knows."

Now, Virgilio was the type of guy who—if he was getting married, he was going to invite everyone. It's just the way he was. He wanted everyone to feel good. He couldn't afford it, though. He may have been a doctor, but nobody had that much money. In fact, there wasn't a place in New York City big enough to hold all the people if he had the wedding there. So he decided to go back home to his village in Calabria to get married. And I set off on my first trip to Italy.

It was something else. The minute I stepped on board the ship, I felt like I was already in Italy. That boat was nothing like the places I'd been to in America. All the people dressed with elegance, and they were always ready to laugh. They were bothered by absolutely nothing. The food was unlike anything in the Italian restaurants in New York. There was music all the time, and all the songs were in Italian. There was one song that a guy sang the first night during dinner, with just a violin, "Al di La." Oh, it was a beautiful song in Italian! I've heard it sung in English, and it's not bad, although it's not quite the same:

Al di la, you are far above me, very far

Al di la, as distant as the lovely evening star

Where you walk flowers bloom, when you smile all the gloom

Turns to sunshine

And my heart opens wide

When you're gone it fades inside

And seems to have died

Al di la, I wondered as I drifted, where you were

Al di la, the fog around me lifted, there you were

In the kiss that I gave was the love I had saved for a lifetime

Then I knew all of you

Was completely mine!

And the way this guy sang it! After he finished I gave him a tip so he'd sing it again. I'd never gotten carried away by a song like that. I guess the romance of Virgilio's wedding, and the knowledge that I'd soon be seeing my father and mother's homeland, stirred something in me. This old-fashioned love song just got to me. Was this the passion that all young couples felt as they started out? The feeling that carried my parents over the Atlantic Ocean from their homeland to make a better life for their family? Who knew? I tipped the singer over and over, until he started performing "Al di La" as soon as he caught sight of me at dinnertime.

The real impact of this trans-ocean voyage hit me when we put into Naples and I stepped out on the deck with all the returning Italians. The throng on the pier roared in greeting; almost everyone on the deck called joyfully back. I was one of the few with no one to meet me. And you know what? It was scary! I had a sudden impression of how it must have been for my father, arriving in America with hardly any money, no knowledge of the language, and no one to help him. The guts he must have had! I thought. Where do I go now? What do I do?

Virgilio had told me to exchange some money right away when I disembarked and call him on a pay phone. He would be staying with a friend in Naples. Fortunately I knew a little Italian.

"*Mi scusi, signore, ma dov'è il telèfono?*"

An elderly man in a straw hat heard my broken Italian and broke into a huge smile. "*Ah, Americano! Qui, qui, eccolo.*"

He took me by my elbow and pulled me to the phone, as if he'd known me all his life.

But none of the money I'd been given seemed to work. It didn't fit. I said to someone else, "*Come fa?*"

In the same strong, familiar way, another man explained about the phone to me. It turned out I was supposed to buy a token for the phone from the *tabbacaio*, the newsstand. I bought a few, put a token in the phone, and dialed. Nothing happened! In fact, I lost the token; I couldn't get it back.

A little old woman came shuffling by with her family: children, grandsons, luggage, everything. She saw me trying to get my token back. "*Che è successo?*"

It took the whole family, shouting and laughing, to show me that I needed to dial the number first, and then put in the right amount of tokens. They hovered around me until I finally got Virgilio, then they yelled their "*buon giornos*" and took their leave.

Virgilio told me to take a cab to a hotel in Naples, and he'd see me for a late supper. The cabbie would know where to go.

A cab? Oh, *Madonn'*, I thought, now what do I do?

It was something else, getting around Italy for the first time. But my fears drifted away once I discovered that anyone who heard my broken Italian wanted to fall over backwards to help me.

A plate of pasta, a glass of wine, a cup of espresso—every bite of lunch seemed full of the same good-natured heartiness that I found in the people. I had never felt so nourished and at ease. I napped in my hotel room, where even the sheets and pillows seemed to be made of different stuff, more wholesome and comfortable, than in the hotels in America.

Late in the evening I walked around the corner to meet Virgilio at a nearby restaurant. He was already there, waving to me. His fiancé was not with him. She didn't want him to see her before their wedding morning at the church, he said.

"Well, listen," I said. "Do you have a song yet for after the wedding? 'Al di La'. I'm telling you, 'Al di La', what a beautiful song!"

He smiled at me blankly. "I don't know it," he said. "No. But the musicians, they will know what to play. They know the songs people will like."

"They'll know it," I assured him.

A few days later, the wedding took place at the church in the main square, the piazza, of Virgilio's hometown, his *paese*, Amaroni. Along the main street, the people of the village hung huge colored swathes of fabric out their windows and off the railings of their terraces. Virgilio told me that these were supposed to be banners, in celebration of his wedding; but he confided that they were actually mostly rugs. The people didn't have the money for real family banners. It didn't matter; the bright rugs were festive, and they hung from every window, a tribute to the prominence of Virgilio's family.

He told me, "We'll—how do you say it, *sfiliamo in corteo*—make like a parade."

"Like a procession."

"Yes, a procession, down the main street to the school yard. The whole *paese*, whoever can spare their furniture, they put out tables and chairs for the party. My family has everything prepared."

"You have the party outside? With people's furniture, outside? But Virgilio, what if it rains?"

He laughed. "Armand, you see the way it is now?" He gestured toward the steeple of the church, which was already showing up bright white in the early morning sun. The sky behind it was as blue as I'd ever seen, without a cloud. Beautiful. "It's like that for another three months."

What an experience! A real experience. Everyone in the village crowded into the church for the wedding. Virgilio's bride was beautiful. Afterward we all walked them down to the schoolyard for the feast, with the musicians from the church following right behind. The whole village shared what they had. I've eaten at many of the best restaurants in Italy and America since then, but even at the fanciest places in New York, there's never been another table where I tasted real bread like that. Real olive oil, wine, cheese and fruit.

I thought of my poor mother and father, of the suffering they went through, and felt happy for them for the first time. Once, they lived in Italy; once, they got married and had a feast like this, with the whole village wishing them well. Look at how long it kept them going.

Back in the States, nobody wanted to hear about Italy. All they wanted to know was, "Armand, what about you? When are you getting married, for crying out loud?"

My sister worried about me. I'd set her up in the house I'd bought, with a renter downstairs. She was tickled to be keeping house, and relieved to be out of the tenements, but she worried about what I was eating, whether I was lonely, the whole bit.

I bought another house, and made a studio apartment for myself upstairs. It was a nice little place. Frankie lived downstairs with his family. He had married a woman with four children. Her husband had run off, the bastard, and Frankie with his heart of gold had married her. It was really Frankie's house. I signed off as the purchaser, but he paid the mortgage, just as Catherine did on the other house. Before long I did the same for Jimmy, who took the house next door, and for Augie, with a little house near Fordham University.

On Sundays, we all continued to gather, with all the nieces and nephews, usually at Catherine's. What a racket the children made! And now the nieces, especially the older ones, getting to be teenagers, were in on the act, too. "Uncle Armand, when are you going to get married?"

"Never mind!" I told them. "Wipe that lipstick off your face. Does your father know you wear lipstick?"

Of course this didn't shut them up. They were modern children. Their parents were soft-hearted, remembering how we grew up. They had no fear of me. They only teased me more.

***

In the summer of 1966, I finally met my future wife. I was at a party with Cesare Cucci, who was about to marry Gilda, a pretty Filipina medical student. Cesare took the opportunity to introduce me to Gilda's friend, Boots, who would be Gilda's maid of honor.

Right away I noticed a difference between Boots and most of the women I got introduced to. She wore very little makeup, for one thing, and she was not holding a cigarette. Although she spoke softly, she was not shy. In fact, we hit it off right away, just as I had with Virgilio, Cesare, and the other professionals in their circle. There was no end to the conversation, no trouble with laughing. But it never occurred to me that I might romantically pursue a physician—an educated, professional woman. It was even further from my mind that she might be interested in me.

Boots, for her part, was apparently disappointed that an American man should be so short. I heard later from Cesare that when Gilda encouraged Boots to go out with me, saying that I looked like Don Ameche, Boots said, "Maybe a cross between Don Ameche and Peter Lorre."

I think she had pictured an American boyfriend who would look like Rock Hudson, with lots of hair and broad shoulders. Or maybe Omar Sharif.

She agreed to a dinner date, though, when Cesare suggested it. The four of us went out the following weekend.

We were sitting in the restaurant, a nice Italian place, when I felt like I had to sneeze. I sneezed a couple of times. Boots looked at me funny and asked me what was wrong.

"I don't know. Sometimes when there are too many flowers or perfumes in a place, it makes me sneeze."

"Maybe you're allergic to women," Boots said.

"Something, I don't know." I sneezed again. I really couldn't help it.

But we started to get along. I learned that her real name was Ofelia. Because she was the youngest, she'd gotten nicknamed "the baby" in Tagalog, *bebot*, which in English became "Boots." We found out that we were both the children of farmers, and that neither of us ever wanted to go near a farm again. We both had stories about our brothers in the War. I told her my brothers had been to the Philippines with the Navy.

"They always told me that the most beautiful women in the world were in the Philippines," I said. I don't know what made me say it. I could see her trying not to smile, saying to herself, get a load of this guy. But then she did smile and I got goose bumps.

And then I sneezed again. If this is going to work out, I thought, I've got to tell her that her perfume stinks.

On our first real date together, that's just what I did. I pulled up outside her apartment building, and got out to open the car door for her. She came up in her high heels, in a Jackie Kennedy-style dress that she wore so well, it would have put Jackie Kennedy herself to shame. And the first thing that happened, when I got back into the car and shut my door, was that I sneezed.

"Boots," I told her, "that perfume stinks."

What an insult to a woman like this. I didn't think about it at the time, because I didn't know any better, but picture a professional young woman, a physician, who was up two hours before work every morning, to shampoo and set her hair. Rather than wait until she had a load of laundry to do, she washed out her undergarments every night, so as to never use the same ones two days in row. Even during the War, when her family lived under a palm-frond hut in the jungle to escape the Japanese, she bathed every day in a river, even in the rain. When she was in college and medical school in Manila, and water was rationed, she would put her wash-basin under a dripping faucet every evening, to fill it for the next day's sponge bath. For such a woman to be told she stinks? What an insult! But even if I had known her better, I'd have had to tell her she was killing me with that perfume.

"That stink happens to be Chanel No. 5," she snapped, "and it costs seventy dollars an ounce!"

"Wait a minute! That's why I bought you this." I pulled out the box, wrapped in nice paper. When she opened it, she was impressed.

"'Le De' by Givenchy! But Armand, this is very expensive!"

"You like it?"

"Oh, yes! This is a very fine perfume!"

"You'll really wear it?"

"Yes."

I tried not to sneeze again, but I couldn't help it. I opened my window a little, just to get me through the evening.

We became a foursome, the Cuccis, Boots, and me. It became my habit on Saturday nights to get dressed in the evening and drive to their place in Manhattan. Bootsie would take the train from Brooklyn. We'd dine at the Cuccis' place, or go out to a restaurant. I'd drive Boots back to Brooklyn at the end of the evening. For the first time in my life, I was really looking forward to Saturday nights. Honest to God, I heard singing — in my head, not on the radio — every time I got in the car with her to go to Brooklyn. She had me hearing "Al di La."

One day, Cesare, Virgilio, and some of my other doctor friends invited me out on a boat. One of them asked me how things were going with Boots.

I didn't know where to begin. Here I was on a boat, actually a yacht, in the Long Island Sound, talking to professional men about a beautiful, educated woman who was really too good for me.

And just like that, I realized that I wanted to marry her. There was no doubt in my mind. It couldn't have been more than three months since we'd met. I'd never even considered such a thing before. But I was sure that I wanted to spend the rest of my life with my Bootsie.

"I don't know what to say," I stammered. "I think I want to marry her. But I'm a nobody. How can I marry a medical doctor?"

My friends erupted in shouting. "How can you think you're not good enough? You can do anything! Any woman would be blessed by God to have you for a husband!"

They didn't really understand my worry. Boots had been brought up in the Philippines, and they were from Italy, but they all had the same kind of background: parents who could give them anything; a familiarity with the best of clothes, food, and educated ideas; a different kind of heritage. My Bootsie was a princess, accustomed to having only the best. I was from the streets of the Bronx, a child of the Depression. How could I provide the kinds of things she had come to expect, and the lifestyle she deserved?

"I can't," I said. "I would destroy her life. I can't be that selfish. It just can't be."

Virgilio actually slapped me. "What's the matter with you? Selfish, a nobody, what kind of nonsense is that? Armand, you are a prince!"

"Virgilio, ow!"

Cesare drew himself up as if he was about to deliver a speech. "Armand," he said with great solemnity, "You are a diamond in the rough."

I was embarrassed, but I now had a little hope.

The next Saturday night, after dinner in Manhattan, I drove Boots home via the Brooklyn Bridge, as usual, going slowly so that we could look out over the harbor at the Statue of Liberty. She never tired of the lights of New York, especially Lady Liberty, shining on the water.

"Isn't she beautiful?" Boots said. She began to recite. "Give me your poor, your weary..."

I had no idea what she was talking about. Maybe that's why I just blurted out the first thing that came into my head. "When we get married, I think March is a good time."

Boots stared at me, but she didn't lose her poise. God bless her, she looked beautiful.

"No way," she said. "I have to write to my parents, and they have to say it's okay. My father won't let me marry a foreigner just like that. The earliest we could get married is May."

"A foreigner?" I repeated. "But I'm not the foreigner, you're the foreigner!"

Boots didn't argue with me, but she held firm. "In any case, I will not marry without my parents' blessing."

When I stopped outside her apartment, opened the car door for her, and kissed her cheek goodnight, I tried once more. "Boots, what if they can't get here in May? Can't you just write and tell them about me?"

"No," she said, and stepped into her apartment building without looking back.

Naturally, her strength of principle made me love her even more.

It was only January. I knew I'd be in a sweat until May. Not Boots, though. She helped choose a menu for the reception; she didn't object when I booked our honeymoon in Jamaica; she even got baptized Catholic so that we could get married in the church. But she would not consider foregoing her parents' blessing. Every now and then I'd let slip, "When we're married, we should such-and-such…"

And she'd answer me, "If we're married, I think it should be this way…"

And then it was May. All the arrangements were finalized. It came time to pick up Bootsie's parents at the airport.

I called them, out of respect, Mr. and Mrs. Esguerra. The father spoke English very well. He was kind of quiet. The mother's English was not so good, but as we drove out of the airport and into New York City, she asked questions through her husband. As I answered, we began to have a conversation. I found out she was not afraid to speak up or speak her mind. Sometimes she'd even shout.

Mrs. Esguerra was less than five feet tall, but she had to weigh over 200 pounds; she was that fat. I found out that she'd been very poor as a child in the Philippines, but that through hard work and discipline she had built up a business, starting with gathering salt from the sea and pressing oil from coconut meat, and ending finally with a store and a mechanic's garage. She had raised five children on the run, while her husband was fighting in World War II. They'd been forced to refugee to different parts of the Philippines because of his record with the Japanese. Mrs. Esguerra had more fight in her than some of these guys from the neighborhood twice her height. We understood very little of each other's words, but we spoke the same language.

Mr. Esguerra was his wife's opposite. He was rail-thin and used few words, even though he understood and spoke English very well. In fact, every time he did speak, he sounded like an encyclopedia. Bootsie told me he used to laugh and joke much more, but he'd gotten quieter after the War. He was a decorated hero, in fact, and a captain in the U.S. Army. He'd led the men under him so effectively that the Japanese blacklisted him, then captured and imprisoned him. He'd been released upon swearing allegiance to Japan, but immediately found the nearest American command center, informed against the Japanese, and began leading guerrilla attacks against them. Once, he'd had to hide in the jungle treetops for three days, watching the Japanese hunt for him on the ground below. I showed him tremendous respect. Over the next week, I took him to see all the veterans' memorials I could think of.

At some point Boots told me that among Filipinos, it would be considered more appropriate for me to call her parents, "Ma and Pa." The subject of canceling the wedding plans never came up. Of course, our first dance was "Al di La."

Above: Our first
house in Rye, NY

Above Left: Boots
and me, covered in
sunburn, in Jamaica

Left: The whole
family, Sept. 1970,
after my lymphoma
diagnosis

An Open Coffin

The Saving Grace of Boiled Rice

Every bride wants her husband to be her knight in shining armor, and every groom wants to place his wife on a pedestal. But that's not life. I had worried, before marrying Boots, that she would one day realize that I was not good enough for her. I soon learned that she never wanted to be on that kind of pedestal. She wanted to be my wife, and that meant not only sticking with me, but fighting with me, and urging me to fight even when I thought I could fight no more. She accepted my faults, but still expected me to be a better person than I even knew I could be. She proved from day one that little chinks in my armor were not going to bother her.

We had booked our honeymoon at Half-Moon Bay in Montego Bay, Jamaica, which in those days was newly established as a posh, refined resort. We had a bungalow, with its own little swimming pool, and a steward, who would serve us meals poolside, whenever we wished to dine privately. A calypso band strolled the grounds, serenading guests throughout the day and evening. This was the perfect 1960s idea of tropical paradise.

One morning, I was taking a nap in the coolness of the bungalow, when I felt my new wife take my hand. It was so pleasant to lie quietly together. I pretended I was still asleep. For the last week she'd been climbing waterfalls, swimming in the ocean, and eating exotic shellfish. Jamaica reminded Boots of the Philippines, her homeland. I couldn't get used to it. I liked the food and the peacefulness, but otherwise I'd been just trying to keep out of the sun. I'd never known the sun could be so strong. It took away my appetite. At times, I felt the beginnings of the old sickness in my stomach. I never said anything to Boots; I didn't want to spoil our honeymoon.

Boots squeezed my hand and let go. I opened my eyes, expecting to see her looking at me with starry eyes, the way she looked at her movie stars. Instead she was looking at me the way a doctor looks at a patient. "What?" I said.

"Your pulse is a little irregular."

"You're taking my pulse?"

"I was going to wake you up for a swim, but you haven't seemed well lately. And when I looked at you sleeping, your breathing made me nervous. So I took your pulse. A little irregular."

"I feel fine!" I insisted.

To prove I wasn't sick, I got up and put on my trunks.

Boots was already in the pool when I came out, swimming like a fish. She'd been swimming all her life, after all. She was wearing a bikini.

"Do your parents know you have a bikini?" I yelled.

She answered with a splash. I jumped back.

"*Madonn'*, it's cold!" The sun was so strong, even though it was not even nine in the morning. How could the pool be that cold?

"Just get in!" she called back to me.

She looked so happy, so pretty. I didn't want to spoil her good time. I stepped into the water at the shallow end, and, as had been my habit, swimming in the Bronx River as a teenager, I splashed a bit on my hands, then rubbed a little water on my chest, to get used to it. I didn't want to lose my breath.

"What are you doing?" she yelled.

"I'm coming, here I come," I said. I held my breath and pushed away from the stairs, swimming toward her with a slow stroke. I swam as I remembered swimming in the Bronx River, moving my arms and legs like a frog.

Boots swam under me and came up on the other side, treading water. "Armand," she said, "Don't we go on the yacht today?"

Yacht! It was a big sailboat, but I wasn't sure it was a yacht. "Ten o'clock," I said.

Just then, our steward came with breakfast. I swam toward the stairs. Even though I had a head start, Boots beat me. She gave me another splash as she got out of the pool.

"Bootsie, don't be so smart!" I said.

We had our breakfast under an umbrella by the pool. Half-Moon Bay had excellent coffee, good eggs, and fruit like I'd never tasted before. I'd never gotten enough fruit when I was a child, except in the summer, when my father's peaches were ripe. I filled up on the papaya, then got sleepy and relaxed back into my chair.

"What time is it?" I asked Boots.

"Almost nine."

"Wake me in twenty minutes, will you, Boots? I'm just going to close my eyes for a minute."

"You're going to sleep? Again?"

"Just for a minute, *cecharell'*, okay? Wake me up." I closed my eyes. Maybe I'd had too much to drink the night before.

When I woke up, it had gotten very hot. The sun was baking my legs; the reflection in the pool nearly blinded me. Boots was gone. I got up and went into the bungalow to get out of the sun. It was cooler there, but my legs were sunburned up to my knees. Even the bottoms of my feet were burned. The clock read 10:30. I'd missed the boat.

Later, Boots told me she'd woken me up, but I'd told her to go without me.

"I didn't say that!" I said. "I wanted to go on the boat!"

"The yacht," she corrected me. "Anyway you probably wouldn't have liked it. It was fun."

"Wait a minute!"

"We had the sun on us for the whole hour, and you had to rush from one side to the other whenever they changed direction. Armand, we were like this!" She held her hand out to show how the boat had tipped from side to side as they turned. "And the spray from the ocean was all over us! Boy, was that exhilarating."

"I got sunburned!"

"You fell asleep in the sun," she shrugged. The way she looked at me, you'd think she left me there on purpose.

We took it easy for the remaining few days of our honeymoon.

We went to the shop of a furniture maker, who turned out to be a little Filipino man with a Jamaican accent. We ordered a mahogany dining set from him, to be shipped to the States.

We took long drives in the country. Boots ruined a pair of white leather sandals, stepping into a cow pasture to relieve herself. She just laughed, and went barefoot the rest of the day.

In the mountains, we visited an old woman who fed hummingbirds from her porch. It was a beautiful vista from there, looking over the ocean. She gave us little cups filled with sugar water, and the hummingbirds came right up to sip from the cups.

I saw black clouds on the horizon, and said I thought it might rain. She said, "Oh no. My rain comes from that way." She gestured the other way, to the clear horizon.

Not a minute later, we heard the boom of thunder. Sheets of water began pouring down over the edge of her porch roof. She laughed right along with us.

Having someone to travel with, in this case my best friend, my wife, gave me something to bring back. I'd had the same experience going to Italy with Virgilio. There was no souvenir better than the memories I brought back. If I'd gone by myself, who would I talk to about it?

When we got back from our trip, we told our stories to Boots' sister, Grace, and their parents, who had all been staying in our apartment while we were away. They smiled and enjoyed the stories, of course, but Boots and I enjoyed them more.

I could even laugh when we told the story of my sunburned feet, over breakfast one Sunday morning.

Boots' mother said something in Tagalog, and they all laughed.

"What?"

Boots said, "Oh, nothing. She just says you're pale."

And they laughed some more.

The rest of the morning passed in this way, as Boots, Grace, and their mother puttered around the kitchen and the apartment, while their father sat and read a book that was thicker than my wrist. I read the paper. The older women were teaching Boots to cook. They made a chicken dish, to save for dinner, and a cake. They made boiled rice. Ever since we'd gotten back from Jamaica, it had been boiled rice with fish, boiled rice with chicken, boiled rice with beef. I'd liked it fine the first time, but I was ready for some pasta. Meanwhile, they were speaking Tagalog all the time, and they never stopped laughing. I wished I could understand what they were talking about. I hated to ask, over and over.

Boots and I were supposed to meet Cesare and Gilda for brunch. I wondered whether Cesare had had experiences like this with Gilda's family.

Finally, it was time to go.

"On a nice day, always go out," I said to my in-laws, as I waited for Bootsie by the door. "Because you're going to get a lot of cold days in New York, and rain."

Boots was hesitant to leave her parents so soon after our return from Jamaica. But it was a beautiful day in New York City, and we were both eager to meet our friends for brunch. It would be our first time out in New York as man and wife.

We met the Cuccis at the Waldorf Astoria, one of the most refined places for brunch in the city. This was the type of thing Bootsie loved, an elegant place and fine food. I loved it too. It had only been in the last few years that I'd come to understand that the most important part of mealtime was not filling your belly.

"So Boots, did he hurt you?" Cesare said, and Boots blushed as the rest of us laughed.

"Never mind!" she said. "Listen to how your macho friend spent his honeymoon."

She told about the waterfalls she'd climbed, the yacht she'd sailed on — while I had slept or sat in the shade. It was now my turn to blush.

Meanwhile, their stories were all about the townhouse they were buying on the Upper West Side. Gilda had all kinds of ideas about antiques for the dining room and living room.

We were standing outside the Waldorf still talking, about to head back to Brooklyn, when Gilda said that they were going to Nyack to look for antiques.

"Why don't you come?" Cesare said to Bootsie and me. "It's a beautiful country village on the Hudson River. A perfect day for a drive."

He was right—it was a perfect day. End of May, before the real hot days of summer. I'd never seen Nyack. It sounded like such a quaint, out-of-the way place.

"We really can't," said Bootsie. "My parents are at home in Brooklyn. We have to go back."

"Oh, come on, Boots, we'll be back early," Gilda said, and Cesare tried to wheedle her too.

But no, she'd promised her sister, she'd promised her mother and father—it struck me, suddenly, that she'd committed us both, unnecessarily. For what? To stay inside on a perfect day? I couldn't even understand when her family talked, most of the time. What was I going to do in the apartment with them this afternoon? And what was I going to eat—boiled rice again?

"Tell you what, I'll go," I said.

Boots was surprised. I could tell by the way she looked at me. She said, "Armand—should I go back to Brooklyn by myself?"

I didn't see that it was a problem. She loved to drive. "Of course you can get back to Brooklyn. You'll be fine."

"We haven't even seen my parents except for a couple of hours."

"I'll be home later. They want to talk to you, anyway, not me."

We walked Boots to the car, and she drove off. I turned around to Cesare and Gilda. "Well, let's go," I said.

I climbed into the narrow back seat of the Cuccis' convertible. It wasn't really big enough for two. Boots and I would have really had to squeeze in.

Cesare put the roof down.

"Cesare, the sun!" I said.

"Armand, I thought you were macho!"

"We'll be fine," Gilda said, laughing.

The sun and the wind were too much. Cesare liked to drive on the highways outside the city. I didn't blame him; they were faster, and it felt good to escape the traffic lights and tall buildings of Manhattan for a glimpse of green countryside. But there was no shade. The day was hotter than we'd thought it would be. We were all parched, and a little sunburned, by the time we pulled into Nyack.

It was fun going into all the little shops. Cesare liked to hear my comments about things. But really, antique shopping was their business.

I imagined the kinds of things Boots would like to buy one day, when we had a house. We both liked antiques, not the junk, but the good, older furniture, the chairs made with heavy, carved, polished wood, and the tabletops made of thick slabs of marble or alabaster. Brass knobs. Porcelain lamps. I almost bought a lamp, but I thought I'd rather just come back with Boots, when we could look together.

We got the best meal we could, later in the evening, at a bar that served hamburgers and sandwiches. What a difference from the Waldorf Astoria!

"I guess this is how they eat in the country!" Gilda said. "Armand, what has Grace been cooking? I bet you've had some fantastic Filipino meals. What are they cooking tonight, do you know?"

"I don't know, some chicken," I said. What a smell there was in the bar, from the grease and the beer.

"We should have eaten in Brooklyn!" Gilda laughed.

I got back home about nine o'clock. Ma and Pa had gone to bed. Boots was in the bedroom with the radio on. Grace was in the kitchen, giving me a dirty look as I came through the door. I didn't get it. Back in the neighborhood, none of the guys had stopped hanging out after they got married. Even the old men, like my father, took their walk on the piazza. You weren't supposed to lose your friends just because you got married.

Before long, it was time for Ma and Pa to go back to the Philippines. Grace went back to her apartment in the Heights.

Boots nervously cooked the first dinner that she'd ever prepared by herself; I'm sure it was a great task for her. I knew she wanted to impress me. She prepared chicken with some brown sauce, and boiled rice.

I looked at this food. Looking back, I am so sorry for what I said, but at the time, I had only one thing in mind: the boiled rice at dinner had to stop.

"Boots," I said, "take a good look at my eyes." I spread the corners apart with my fingers. "See this? I'm not Oriental. I'm of Italian descent and was brought up on pasta and bread."

My poor wife. Not a word from her.

I didn't go on. I felt a little ashamed, even though I thought I was only saying what was right. She forgave and forgot, because she was too warm-hearted to ever hold a grudge. And I, with my macho background, convinced myself that she would say something if it really bothered her.

This is one of the things that made our marriage succeed. Neither of us ever held grudges. I've heard people say it's hard to adjust to being married, but for us there was nothing to it. We were good company. And she never bossed me around. No way. In my mother's house, if I got caught lying down on the couch, Ma would scream. "Get up!" With Boots, if I was tired, it didn't bother her. She was too sure of herself to let little things get to her.

One thing that I couldn't get used to was Boots' working life. It got me anxious. I'd been around doctors for years at this point, and I'd always known they worked very hard, but I hated seeing the long hours Boots worked, hearing the phone ring in the middle of the night when she was on call, sometimes waiting up until early the next morning before she could come home, or call, to say she was all right.

It wasn't long before we found out Boots was pregnant. I thought at first that she'd cut back on working, but she didn't. She said she didn't feel sick, and that running up and down the hospital stairs was good for her. Sometimes she was visibly tired, but when I urged her to rest, she'd say, "Oh, no. I'll take a nap at the hospital."

Of course I worried, but thought she must know best. She was a doctor, after all.

At the same time we learned that the arrival of the mahogany dining set we'd ordered in Jamaica would be delayed. That was all right; we didn't have much of a dining room yet, anyway. We started looking for an apartment with more space, something with a third bedroom for the baby.

We found a new place earlier than expected, a beautiful 10th floor apartment: three bedrooms, living and dining rooms, and a butler's pantry. Parquet wood floors throughout, except for the linoleum in the kitchen. From the living room, you could see Prospect Park, and from the dining room, New York City. We ate in the kitchen for now. Over the next couple of weeks, we started to slowly furnish the apartment: green Oriental rugs for the living room, red for the dining room. We ordered a sofa.

Furnishing the place took a long time, because Boots could only come with me on weekends to choose things. I wouldn't do it alone, although my schedule was more flexible than hers, for fear of picking something she didn't like. With the hours she worked, there were some weeks I hardly saw her at all.

***

One morning, before it was light, I woke up to hear Boots calling me from the bathroom. I found her crouched by the toilet, cupping something in her hands. "Armand," she said, "A cup of water."

"What is it?" I was still half-asleep.

"Water. Just get me a cup of water."

I grabbed the cup by the sink, filled it, and handed it to her. She immediately poured it over her cupped hand. She put down the cup and made the sign of the cross.

"Boots, what's wrong? Is it the baby?"

She started to cry. "He was alive," she said. "He came out alive."

It had only been a minute since I came into the bathroom. I now saw the blood in the little bit of light coming through the window. Before Boots would let me help her, she made me find a box for the baby. From her nightstand, I took the little cardboard box where she kept her rosary. She laid him on the cotton, a tiny thing, maybe two inches long. I looked away. I couldn't imagine how she'd known he was alive. We cleaned her up, and I found something warm to wrap her in, so we could go to the hospital.

In the car, I asked her, "How did it happen?"

"I don't know," she said, still crying. She sounded so much more tired than she had when I first walked in the bathroom. "I just had to go to the bathroom, and I had this feeling—so I caught him. He was alive. I had to baptize him. Robert."

That was the name we had picked for a boy.

Later, in the hospital, the doctors told us that there was no clear reason for the miscarriage. Boots was healthy. They said she was probably pushing herself too hard.

"You see!" I said to her, as we settled her in the hospital for the night. "Lifting patients that are too heavy for you, doing x-rays—"

"I have a lead apron when I do those."

"Never mind!"

"A fifty-pound lead apron. Maybe it's too heavy. And maybe-running up and down the stairs…"

"That's right! Thank God you didn't hurt yourself."

"But when there's a code—you can't take the elevator, you won't get there in time. That's what the work demands."

"That's exactly it! The work! You have to take it easy."

There was no question that for the first couple of weeks, Boots couldn't work. But within the month she was working again. From the hours she was keeping, I didn't think she'd even slowed down. In fact, as the weeks passed, I thought she was working more. It was as if she didn't hear me urging her to cut back, no matter how I scolded, "Do you want to get yourself sick?"

I tried to help by taking her out to dinner so she wouldn't have to cook. Once, we went to Catherine's house for Sunday dinner, and there she learned how to make my mother's gravy. She was getting to be a good cook. She could make pasta, beef, chicken, any kind of roast. She got a kick out of it. But I insisted that we eat out at least twice a week. With the schedule she kept, she needed a break.

The next couple of months passed, and the weather turned cool. We'd been married almost six months. One Sunday, I planned a drive out to Long Island with Virgilio, for dinner at his brother's house. I was happy for the invitation. I felt we hadn't seen friends in a long time.

"Armand, you go," Boots said. "I'm too tired. I need to rest for work tomorrow."

"Come on, Boots!" I said. "This way you won't have to cook!"

"I have leftovers. I don't need to cook. You go. They're your friends."

"That hospital is wearing you out," I said. We didn't talk about the miscarriage much anymore, but she knew how I felt. I blamed her job for the loss of the baby.

I went to Long Island alone with Virgilio.

Virgilio's sister-in-law was a great Italian cook. We had a wonderful time talking about Italy — what else? The last time I'd been there had been before I got married. I'd been meaning to take Boots. But again, her work schedule wouldn't allow it.

Virgilio's brother and his wife were planning a trip in two weeks. They were getting a good deal on the tickets, too.

"Armand, why don't you come?"

"Sure, I will!" I said, without thinking. I put the dates in my calendar, and they promised to book my flight with theirs.

I didn't wake Boots when I got home that night. But at breakfast in the morning I said, "Boots, how about a trip to Italy?"

After she heard the dates, she said, "Armand, I can't go then. I can't get a week off just whenever I want. Can't we go later — in maybe two months?"

"All the arrangements are made," I said. "I can't cancel my ticket."

"You really want to go?"

"Yeah, I really do. It's a good deal."

"Are you really going to leave me here alone?"

I suddenly understood how disappointed she was. She'd heard me talking with my friends about Italy since before we were married. And she would probably be lonely in Brooklyn, with thoughts of the baby in the back of her mind.

"No! Of course I don't want to leave you alone," I said. "Boots, let me see what Virgilio's brother says tomorrow."

The next day I got word about the trip. It really was a good deal, too good to pass up, I thought.

When I talked to Boots about it, she said, "Well, if it's that good of a good deal – go, I guess."

I felt torn about leaving Boots, but passing up Italy on the cheap seemed like too much of a loss. Looking back, I think I was just showing off, parading my own independence. What macho crap!

"We'll go together soon," I said.

She smiled at me. "I know."

A week later I was on the plane, wondering what I was doing, going to Italy without my Bootsie. What in the world was I trying to prove? That I would not be controlled by her vacation schedule? I guess I let the airlines take charge of me instead, by falling for cheap prices advertised during the off-season. The Ciampas were very nice people, and we ate well and had some laughs. But we had never really socialized much, except through Virgilio. I didn't know them, and probably wouldn't see them much after we got back to New York. Who was I going to share this trip with? Who would remember it with me?

The week went by in a blur. All I could think about was Boots. I wondered what she was doing, whether she was feeling well, whether she missed me. She had just lost her first child, after all. Our child. What had I been thinking, to leave her alone? I tried to call once, timing it so that I could get her before she went to work in the morning. But the connection was terrible. It was just good enough for her to hear me when I yelled, "I love you," and for me to hear her yell it back.

When I arrived in New York, I couldn't wait to get back to Brooklyn. Virgilio's brother urged me to come out for dinner, but I insisted that I must get home, even though I knew Boots wouldn't be finished with work for hours.

Waiting for me at the apartment was the mahogany table and chairs from Jamaica, all set up in the dining room. It was a unique set—Queen Anne chairs with extra-broad backs and wide cushions, the table expandable to seat ten people, but collapsed now into a four-person circle. The bottom was carved with four lions, opening their mouths to roar. Boots had put on a tablecloth, one that her parents brought from the Philippines for our wedding. It was white and edged with flowers of different colors. She was still out, as I'd known she would be. I put away my things and went out to run some errands.

When Boots returned I had the record player on, playing the Al Martino recording of "Al di La".

"Welcome home!" I called out, coming to her at the door.

"Hi," she said, taking my kiss. "Did you have a good time?"

"Terrible."

She laughed. "Really! Why?"

"Let's talk about it later. Come in and sit down, look what I did."

On the dining room table, I had placed an anchovy pizza and a bottle of wine.

"So you wouldn't have to cook," I said.

"Very nice!" she said. "How did you know I have something important to tell you?"

"What?"

She sat down and helped herself to a slice of pizza, as I poured her wine. "I'm pregnant again."

I almost stained her mother's tablecloth with the wine.

"Now," she said, "Tell me about your terrible time in Italy."

"I'll never do it again," I said. "I really mean it. Never. Are you feeling all right?"

"Perfect."

"What about the job?"

"I'll modify it."

"Boots."

"I'm not going to lose this baby." She meant it.

Throughout that winter and into spring, I don't know how many times I went out for anchovy pizza in the middle of the night. Sometimes I woke up to find Boots in the kitchen eating an ice cream with Bosco syrup for breakfast. I didn't care. All the women agreed, from my sister and Boots' sisters, to her mother across the Pacific ocean, and even Boots' doctor: she should eat whatever the baby wanted. And the baby kept growing.

***

Donna Lee was born on July 13, 1968. I knew we were not going to raise our family in Brooklyn. Boots didn't like me calling our beautiful home, with three bedrooms, a butler's pantry, and parquet floors, a tenement. But to me, an apartment was a tenement.

In any case, Boots agreed. The baby had begun to stand on her own, and her favorite thing to do was to pull up on the sill of the living room window. She would gaze forever at Prospect Park, where she took walks with the wonderful woman who watched her while Boots and I were at work. To us it seemed pitiful. We couldn't bear to see our baby trapped inside like this. Now that we had started our family, it was time to buy a house.

We made looking at property, all over the suburbs, part of our weekend excursions. Long Island was like a trap, only one way in and out; North Salem was too far; Mamaroneck, New Rochelle, and Mount Vernon were all nice neighborhoods, but none were quite right. The homes were lovely, but they were right on top of each other. We wanted some space.

We finally found an old farm in Rye, New York, that had been subdivided. The main house was available, but I bought the gardener's cottage, which was on a whole acre. It felt even bigger, because the back yard was bordered not by other homes, but by the golf course. There were also a carriage house, two chalets and a stable on the cottage property. I found out that the stables and carriage house had sheltered escaped slaves traveling on the Underground Railroad. I offered to donate the buildings to the town as historical sites. But in those days, they said they didn't know what to do with something like that. Imagine what they'd say now!

We bought the property, and got to work on the gardener's cottage right away. Within a few months, you'd never have believed it was ever a little house. We added a dining room, a huge living room, a master suite, three bedrooms upstairs, and two more bathrooms. In the original upstairs bathroom, there was an old bathtub, the kind with claw feet. We left that in for Donna Lee to have her bath. She had all her toys in the original main room downstairs, which we made into a family room.

I'd never been so happy. Boots was busier than ever, not only working, but also teaching. She became the associate director of anesthesia at nearby Grasslands Hospital, part of New York Medical College. I couldn't believe I'd ever wanted her to stop working. Every day she saved lives. Every day she proved to be what a physician should be, a wise, caring, educated person who put her patients first. I was so proud of her.

Meanwhile, I had my real estate office in the Bronx. The deals came more easily now. I was involved in building deals, some of which I had to fight for—whether it was the boards in charge of approving the work, or the contractors who dragged their feet. But I felt like I'd really made it.

Every day, leaving my house, I passed the country club, where I saw young boys and girls at the swimming pool and golf course, having a wonderful time. I felt jealous at first, thinking I had lost my childhood, and could never make it up. Then I thought of my own children. I could make it up, by giving them the best and enjoying it with them.

By the end of 1969, my life was underway with a wonderful wife and a daughter in a beautiful home. In February of 1970, Boots gave me more wonderful news: later that year, we were to have a second child. What else was there but to enjoy life and live it well?

But with the good comes the bad. So it happened with me. Life, they say, begins at 40. There had been a movie with that title when I was a struggling young man, and I always thought my life would begin at 40. Well, I was barely 41 when my life began to end, with chills and fever.

***

In April of 1970 I caught a springtime cold that just wouldn't go away. For weeks, it seemed, I'd been getting up in the morning with a chill. I didn't tell Boots, at first. She was working 70-80 hours a week and still getting a hot dinner on the table for the baby and me. She never missed an evening. I didn't want to add to her stress, especially with the pregnancy.

Then one evening, we saw the Cuccis for dinner. Gilda served a wonderful meal that I could barely eat.

"Armand," Cesare said, "You're losing weight."

Boots looked at me like she had in Jamaica, the time I'd caught her checking my pulse. Then she and Cesare glanced at each other.

She said, "You're right. I don't think I've really looked at him in a long time."

"I haven't been very hungry," I said. "In fact, I think I have a cold."

"Chills?"

"Fever?"

"How long?"

They bombarded me with questions. I couldn't tell them much.

The next week, my ankles swelled so badly that it was painful to wear my shoes. This time, I didn't try to hide it. I'd had enough of trying to do everything on my own. I'd done that in the years after I got sick in the Army.

I let Boots take me to the hospital for a blood test. That blood test led to another one; and then they did what Boots called "a complete workup."

No answers came from this workup. Everybody was worried, but we had no clear idea of what to do, so we reached out in all directions, pumping our doctor friends and even their friends for information and referrals.

I seemed to get weaker every day. I couldn't eat well, and I kept getting chills. One of my doctor friends suggested that I go to Montefiore Hospital in the Bronx, a top research hospital. When they didn't find anything at Montefiore, another friend got me into Lenox Hill Hospital in Manhattan. It was very tough, going through so many different tests. I was about to be discharged without any answers, when an internist discovered something in my intestines. I heard Boots talking to Cesare about it on the phone.

"It looks like Armand may have lymphoma."

I heard Cesare's voice rise on the other end, but I couldn't hear his words.

Boots said, "Malignant? I don't know. But yes, that's what I thought too."

At almost the same time, September 6, 1970, Delia Grace was born. I thought my wife, being the associate director of anesthesia at Grasslands, would get the best care, but they made all kinds of mistakes. They waited too long to give her anesthesia, and when they did, they put the needle in the baby's head. Thank God she was not poisoned or hurt. The *cecharell'*! She had a thick, black head of hair, just like her mother. And I swear, she smiled from the moment she was born. I only had those first newborn glimpses of her, though. Just after Boots came home with her, I got sent to the hospital for surgery.

I had my first operation on the day before Thanksgiving of 1970. It turned out to be a disaster. The doctor had a great reputation, but was constantly in a rush. He removed 17 inches of my intestines, leaving me with machines to do the rest of the work. He examined me each morning, asked, "Did you pass any gas?" and left until the next day.

I was in pain and constipated, but the nurses were unable to give me anything without orders from my doctor. He was still too busy to see me. I was still suffering when I was sent home.

I got no better, and Boots could see it. I got thinner and thinner, and the pain still got very bad.

It was so unbearable one day that I called my brother Augie. He rushed me to the hospital in his tow truck. We waited and waited. It was very cold in the waiting room. We could hear people in another room, having a Christmas party, laughing, and having a good time. Meanwhile, I was doubled over.

My brother finally blew his top. He burst into the party room. "But what are you people, doctors and nurses or socialites?" he cried. "Is this a hospital or a bar?"

A couple of nurses hurried, red-faced, out of the party to take care of me. I was admitted to the hospital again.

The doctor with the great resume wasn't to be had again. I thought I heard the new doctor tell my wife that I had an intercession. But I was mistaken: intercession is from the angels and saints; if you're lucky, they make a special appeal to God for you, and God gives you grace. My diagnosis was intususception, meaning that my intestines had telescoped in on themselves. Intususception. What a crazy word for your intestines tying themselves into knots.

"Nothing can get through," she explained to my brother, when he came to visit. "It's very painful."

I agreed silently. I could not speak through the pain, not even with the medication they began to give me around the clock.

"He doesn't tell me anything!" she said, almost in tears, my good, good wife. "How is he going to get the right help if he doesn't say anything until the last minute?"

She brought my babies to see me. My two-year-old came to me, with big eyes in her thin little face, her hair too long and her pigtails crooked. She looked so worried. How could a little thing like her know enough to worry?

They tried all different methods of treating the intususception, even putting a nine-foot-long tube, with a balloon at the end of it, through my nose into my intestines. My primary doctor was too busy to do the procedure, and did not even observe the intern he sent. The intern was afraid. I had to coax him to put the tube into my nose.

I went into surgery again to correct the first doctor's mistake. Boots insisted there was no mistake. This was one of the possible complications in a case like mine, she said. But I never forgot that this great doctor couldn't take the time to see me when I was in pain. They corrected the intususception, and I left the hospital very weak.

In a short while I was definitively diagnosed with cancer, lymphoma, that word that my wife had said on the phone to Cesare. No one told me much about it, but they whispered it to each other as if it was a death sentence. My friends, all professionals, had gotten me the best treatment they could find, but at the word "lymphoma," everyone had become mystified.

I had to move on to the next stage of my treatment. Virgilio, especially, insisted. "Boots, lymphoma is the equivalent of a stage-four Hodgkin's…"

"I understand that he has to have radiation," Boots said. "But does it have to be so far away? Why not Lenox Hill?"

Delia, the baby, was four months old. I'd only held her once or twice. And now, they wanted to send me to Bethesda, Maryland for the rest of my treatment.

Virgilio said, "The NIH—that's the only place they give this level of radiation."

And that was it. Arrangements were made for me at Bethesda Hospital in Maryland, at the National Institutes of Health, a government hospital, strictly for research. No one paid, no matter how much money they had.

I was admitted as one among five hundred patients. Caring for us were 15,000 doctors, nurses, other hospital workers, fundraisers, and volunteers, of all races and genders, all looking for answers, looking for a way to comfort and cure. I had been frightened by the cancer. Now there were all these people around me, who believed they could help me battle it and win. I prepared to fight.

I underwent experimental levels of cobalt radiation treatment, at higher levels than they had ever used. I went through more blood tests and all different kinds of tests, besides. It was devastating. The worst part about the tests was the feeling of being violated. But the doctors and nurses didn't like it any better than I did.

I drove home on weekends, 260 miles from the hospital, then returned to the hospital for my cobalt treatment on Monday morning. I didn't mind it. At least I could see my wife and children! They were what I was fighting for. I just couldn't let go; they needed me. The treatment just had to be endured.

When I was finally discharged from Bethesda, I was 92 pounds, just skin and bones. They gave me a good-bye gift of a special foam pillow, for my behind. I'd gotten so thin that it hurt to sit down.

Five hours later, I dragged myself through the door of my house in Rye, and who should meet me at the door but the babysitter, with my baby Delia Grace in her arms. I always thought of this baby as smiling, from the moment she was born, but now she studied me seriously.

"There's Papa," the babysitter said.

My baby girl looked me right in the eye, her expression very solemn, for just a second. And then her whole face spread out in a toothless smile! She knew me! Her chubby legs kicked. Her hands flapped together in front of her as if she were trying to clap. I dropped everything to sit on the couch, so that the babysitter could put her in my arms. Donna Lee climbed up beside me, and kissed my face.

That's how Boots found us a little while later, when she came home from work. Then the babysitter took pictures of all of us. Delia never stopped smiling. Thank God, I was finally home.

"It's finished," I said to Boots.

"I hope so, Armand."

"Oh, it is. Now I just have to get my strength back."

***

One morning a week later, I noticed I was bleeding in the shower. It came from my mouth, and it didn't stop. I bled so much that I almost fainted. I managed to get out and call Boots, who wanted to take me straight to the hospital.

"No," I said. "Wait. Let me catch my breath."

She laid me down and cleaned me up, as the bleeding slowed and stopped. What can be done? I thought. Where can I go, who can I see?

"Armand, please let me take you to the hospital. Grasslands, it's right here."

"Boots," I said. "They can't do anything for me here. Let me rest a little, and then I'll go back to Bethesda."

"Bethesda!"

"Boots, I'm dying. It's simple. I have to go back to Bethesda, even if I have to undergo radiation again. They're the only ones who can help me. If I can be helped."

Boots tried to talk me out of the drive.

"You want to die? You're going to pass out and die right on the New Jersey Turnpike!" she warned me.

"Boots, let me go," I said. "I have no strength, but I can drive. I just have to aim the car."

In then end, I did just that. I got in my car, put my pillow underneath my bottom, and aimed for the hospital, 260 miles away.

I was driving on the New Jersey Turnpike, thinking back on my life, and all the different happenings, when I saw the sign for the Lombardi rest area. I thought about stopping, but I kept going.

A flatbed truck entered the Turnpike from the rest stop. It had five coffins strapped on top. I looked at them, wondering if one of those coffins would be for me. Just then, the strap on the truck snapped. One of the coffins fell off and almost hit my car. The lid opened up at the first bounce, right in front of me. I couldn't even swerve to avoid it. It bounced to the side, and as I looked back through my rear view mirror, I saw the coffin breaking apart on the Turnpike. I thought, did it open up to let me out, or let me in?

I arrived at the hospital very weak. I just drove up to the entrance and called for someone, anyone, to help me. An orderly rushed over with a wheelchair. I don't know what happened to my car.

I'll never forget the music I listened to at Bethesda, that evening after I arrived. I'd just had an examination, and was waiting on a bed for the doctor to come. The music was classical, I guess, but the tune wasn't anything I recognized. It was soothing. I felt myself going to sleep. I felt good, for the first time in a long time.

I daydreamed that I was back in Jamaica, with Boots holding my hand. The sun was warm, not hot. It was a relief, because I'd been cold for months now. I realized that Boots was taking my pulse.

I woke up to find that the music had stopped, and a nurse had come to take my pulse. I wished she wouldn't wake me up. At least I still felt warm and comfortable. The nurse felt my wrist, then picked up my other wrist. She began touching me all over, roughly. I heard her speaking very loudly, although I couldn't understand what she was saying. I wanted to tell her she was being too rough and too loud, but I didn't want to wake up. I felt too good.

Suddenly, I was surrounded by doctors and nurses with all kinds of instruments, all yelling. I became irritated; they were hurting me. They yanked the covers off me, so that I began to shake with the cold.

I finally spoke up. "What's the matter?" I said. "I was feeling so good, and you woke me up."

They all stared at me. "What's the matter?" I said again.

My doctor told me, "We thought you were dead."

It wasn't many days later that I was discharged from Bethesda for the last time. I was no longer bleeding, and I had a little more strength. But I knew I was dying. I didn't want to die in the hospital.

The doctors asked me to have one more test done, something else for my intestines. I could only think that if I stayed any longer, I'd die in the hospital, and then my wife and children would have the burden of getting me out of there. I told them, "Please, leave me alone."

Back in New York, Cesare and Virgilio wouldn't let me give up. They found out about the tests I refused at Bethesda, and coaxed me into an x-ray at Virgilio's brother's office.

The x-ray showed three nodules on my intestines. They took the x-rays to Sloan-Kettering Cancer Center in New York City. The gastroenterologist at Sloan-Kettering, after looking at my intestines again, also suggested taking the test I'd refused at Bethesda. I was around 90 pounds, and no stronger than when I'd been discharged from the NIH. I wished they would leave me alone to die. But my wife urged me to take this one last test. For her, and for my daughters, I did it.

The new doctor put another tube down my throat, to look at the nodes on my intestines. It wasn't more than an hour later that he sat down with me in a waiting room. "I feel very sorry for you, Mr. Miele," he said.

"I want no more operations, doctor. Leave me alone."

The doctor shook his head and continued. "You are of Italian descent, aren't you?"

"Yes."

"You eat a lot of pasta, a lot of bread."

"Yes."

"Mr. Miele, I'm afraid you can't eat those things anymore."

I thought about that for a moment. Why would he tell a dying man what to eat and what not to eat?

"Doctor, are you saying that's my problem, the pasta and the bread?"

He told me that I had a condition called sprue. Eating bread and pasta was tearing up my intestines, so that I could not get nutrition from anything I ate. This was why I couldn't regain my weight and strength. If I went on eating wheat flour, yes, I'd probably die, very soon.

"What are you saying, that if I stop eating flour, I'll get well?"

"I think so, Mr. Miele. It's quite likely. I'm sorry about the pasta."

"Sorry! Sorry? Doctor, please just tell me one thing. What do I eat instead?"

***

What else? Boiled white rice.

My wife put me on a gluten-free diet. I ate boiled white rice with my lunch and dinner every day. In a week, one of the nodes seen on Virgilio's brother's x-ray had disappeared. I gained weight. It didn't take long for the other nodes to disappear too.

Within the month, I got a letter from the NIH, saying they'd received the results from my Sloan-Kettering tests. The letter explained the NIH's research on sprue, and told me that if I participated in a study, the results would be very valuable to the health of others like me. The letter included a plane ticket. I went down to Bethesda not just that time, but twice more. They took blood tests, monitored my recovery, and wrote an article about the whole story.

Sprue came to be known as "celiac disease." Over the next 30 years, the NIH developed a multimillion-dollar institute for research of digestive diseases that was funded in part because of my case. Nowadays, just about anywhere in the United States, you can go to a restaurant or a grocery store and find food that is "gluten-free for celiacs."

So now I know for sure, my marriage was made in heaven. God was good to me when he gave me my wife. I love rice, and I love my wife.

Top Left and Right:
Boots and I enjoy
New Year's Eve, 1984
with Renato Mauro
and long-time
companion, Marina.

Above: The family
mausoleum, 1992

Left: The whole
family at a wedding
banquet, 1990

The Battle to Breathe

Boots Saves Me Again and the Ultimate Loss

I had a good marriage, my health, and two daughters. Those girls surprised me, a man who had grown up with so many brothers, and how proud they made me! My wife and I became financially successful enough to provide comfort and stability for our family. But life is not about comfort and stability, no matter how good you think things are. Life, with all its joys and its tragedies, doesn't let you retire until you retire for good.

In December of 1984, I took my family to Rome for a winter holiday trip—our first away from home. New Year's Eve, we went to a party on the top floor of the Hotel Eden, where we shared *risotto con tartufi e champagne* with a Roman friend, Renato, and his long-time companion, Marina. A couple of weeks before, we had celebrated my 56th birthday.

The windows of the hotel overlooked crooked old streets. Nearby were the famous Spanish Steps. The great Roman park, the Villa Borghese, was visible from the roof in the daytime. Every now and then from the rooftops, someone sent off fireworks that we could see through the windows surrounding the dining room. My girls, aged 16 and 14, sipped wine and laughed at Renato and me in our yellow and red party hats, favors given out by the hotel. Boots would never wear a hat like that. Instead, she and Marina blasted away on tin horns we'd been given to bring in the new year.

Looking back, I think that the early years of my 50s marked the first time in my life that I had no worries. I didn't worry whether I had enough money in my pocket, and my worries about my health were past. I'd had no strange bleeding since the lymphoma and sprue resolved, some 15 years before. I liked to tell people that at 40 I nearly died, so my life had begun at 50.

Boots had taken a position with Ramapo Anesthesiologists, at Good Samaritan Hospital in Suffern. The job moved us out of Westchester into Rockland, and made it possible for us to travel. She worked a minimum of 72 hours a week at all hours of the day and night, which I still worried about, but she also got seven weeks of vacation every year. We had been to Italy so many times that I'd lost track of where we went which year. Rome, Florence, Venice, Spoleto, Perugia, Bari, Via Reggio, and Assisi were some of the more famous places. But there had been a hundred other small towns too, each with its own olive oil, its own wine, its own special building or piazza, and once, an olive tree that was supposed to be older than Jesus Christ. It looked it. We had traveled the United States as well, twice by car and twice by motor home: Chicago, St. Louis, Las Vegas, San Francisco, Miami, Yellowstone, the Grand Canyon, Mount Rushmore, Niagara Falls, the Atlantic and Pacific coasts, and Hawaii. A couple of times, we had even taken the children to the Philippines to see Boots' family.

I had gotten into small-scale commercial real estate development, although the headaches I encountered should have been enough to discourage anyone.

First, I built medical offices for a group of doctors in Yonkers. The group had made me a partner, in return for my construction of the building, but there were a few who got greedy. They hated to share profits with a "non-professional" man. Whenever there was a meeting, one of them spoke against me, and in the end, the group refused me my share of the profits. I got sick with lymphoma and the sprue before I could do anything about it.

The second fiasco was in 1978, when I bought the building in Nanuet that would become my Rockland office. I went to the Clarkstown Planning Board, seeking approval to convert the former inn to an office building. I figured there would be nothing to it, since there was a big mall going up right next door, and most of the buildings in the neighborhood were commercial. But the planning board stopped me and insisted on more detailed building plans. They made it tough, calling me back for hearings again and again. It wasn't until I finally got the approval that one of the board members, who became friendly with me, told me the board had been afraid that I was a racketeer. Because I was Italian, and from the city, they immediately thought, "Mafia."

I had come to learn that all these headaches were part of the cost of doing business. With patience and guts, I overcame them. Even on the medical building, there was still a chance I might get my share. I had found a lawyer, who told me that even after almost 20 years, he could do it for me. I told myself, if he was ready for the fight, so was I. In a way, the so-called professionals and bureaucrats, by trying to put me down, only contributed to my success. By trying to stop me, they made me fight harder. As long as I had my health, I could fight anything.

At times like New Year's Eve on top of the Hotel Eden, though, I could almost imagine a life without fighting, someday, when Boots and I got to be very old. What is the point of life, I thought, if not to enjoy yourself while you can? My daughter Donna Lee had turned 16 that year. At home, I hardly saw her anymore. She was always either in her room with a book, or out with her friends. That New Year's night, she was laughing, relaxed, happy to be with the family for a little while longer. Delia was 14. Everything she did provoked us into laughing, screaming, or crying. She reminded me so much of my mother, never content unless there was excitement in the room. With two minutes to go until midnight, in a banquet hall filled with Italians drinking wine, she was perfectly happy. Boots took a million pictures of the girls making faces, and of Renato and me posing in our hats, trying to look serious.

The waiters got suddenly very busy, pouring Prosecco for the New Year's toast.

"Do they do a countdown here?" Donna Lee asked, picking up her glass and looking around, to see what the people at the other tables were doing.

"Duh, Don," said Delia, "This is Italy. Countdowns are too new-fangled for them."

"Clocks aren't new-fangled," Donna Lee said. Her sister's teasing could still upset her, even at 16. She began to give a lecture on the history of clocks. How did she remember things like that?

"Egghead," said Delia.

In their argument they almost missed the first moment of the New Year. Delia was right; there was no countdown. Instead, the maître'd called for the other waiters to go around to the tables and start shouting, throwing streamers and confetti. We joined in, along with the hall full of Italians.

"Happy New Year! *Buon capo d'anno!*"

We all exchanged kisses, and last of all I kissed Boots, who put her arms around me.

"Ewww, stop that!" said Delia, and I looked over to see her and her sister giving us dirty looks.

"Ha, ha!" I told them, and gave my wife another kiss.

Donna Lee said, "Look!"

She wasn't talking about the kissing, though. She pointed out the nearest windows. All around us, from hundreds of rooftops at once, the Romans were sending off fireworks to welcome the New Year. The light from it was almost blinding.

We waited until the fireworks died down. We had a little ice cream, a little espresso. A little more wine.

"This is how it's done," I told Boots, as I filled her glass. "*Così, e fatt'.*"

"*Buono! Buono!*" she said.

Walking back to our hotel, Boots and I let the girls go ahead of us a few steps. We pretended we'd forgotten the way. We giggled behind them like kids.

The next morning, Boots and the girls wanted to take me to the Vatican for mass. I thought they were kidding.

"We went to church last week," I said, keeping my eyes closed.

"That was for Christmas," Boots said.

Donna Lee added, "Don't you want to see the Pope for New Year's?"

Delia was already running a blow dryer and spraying junk in her hair. I sat on the edge of the bed for a moment before finding my way to the bathroom. I coughed hard against a feeling in my chest, a weight, like phlegm that needed to come up.

"Damned cigarettes," I said. I'd never noticed so many Italians smoking before last night. Renato said it was stylish. Smoking showed that they had money to spend.

At the Vatican I slept through most of mass, and then Boots and the girls wanted to climb the stairs to the *duomo*.

"All the way up there?" I said. I looked at them climbing ahead of me. The walls were close together, the stairs steep, almost like a ladder. They curved around so that you couldn't see to the top.

I started climbing, and counting steps. I couldn't help it. By the time I had counted to 50, we were still nowhere near the top. My legs felt fine, but my head began to spin a little. I thought it was from drinking too much wine the night before. I coughed again against the heaviness in my chest, which was making it harder to breathe in the narrow stairway.

"Donna Lee, Delia!" I called, as I stopped to rest. "Are you crazy, climbing all these steps? Do you know how many steps you climbed?"

"No, Pop," came the answer. They weren't interested.

I kept climbing, counting aloud. "Sixty, sixty-one, sixty two..."

"Pop!"

"Armand! Cut that out!"

"All right." I kept counting to myself, though. I counted to 100. I felt as if I'd been holding my breath underwater. No matter how I tried to breathe, fast, slow, it seemed I couldn't get enough air. Or I couldn't get rid of the bad air. I wasn't sure which.

"Boots," I called. I stopped climbing.

Boots looked back. Then she started back down toward me with that doctor's look.

"What's the matter, Armand?"

"You go," I told her, soft, so the girls couldn't hear. "I can't make all those steps. The air..."

I shook my head. I couldn't explain what was wrong with the air, but it had to be something. I couldn't breathe. Was I claustrophobic?

"Your nose is blue," she said. She picked up my hands, looked at my fingertips, and frowned. "We can all come down with you."

"No, I'll be fine, I'll go slow," I said. "You stay with the girls. Go take some pictures for me."

After watching me take a few breaths, convinced that I was feeling better, Boots turned and followed the girls up the stairs. I made it back down to the bottom. I coughed. Nothing came up.

It felt as if I, myself, had been smoking. I remembered how a cigarette used to make my chest burn. It used to be, when I was a kid, you smoked because the bigger kids smoked, or because the guys in the movies smoked, the tough guys. I thought it made me look tough, too. I was only about 10 years old when I picked up my first cigarette, and I smoked for over 20 years. I only quit, cold turkey, when the government started to publicize the research about smoking being bad for your health. My father died of lung cancer. I'm sure it was the cigarettes.

My wife watched me like a hawk for the rest of the time in Italy. She asked about my breathing, listened to my chest, felt my hands. Even after we got back to New York, she didn't let up.

"What does it feel like?" she'd say. "Shortness of breath, heaviness in the chest? Pain? Weakness?"

"Yes. No, I feel fine now."

"I mean when you exert yourself."

"Oh, then, yes. I can't breathe. But not always. Usually I'm fine."

Then she'd take my pulse and squint at me, and leave me alone for a little while. But whenever I started to exert myself, she made a fuss. At the airport in New York, as I loaded the car with our luggage, she told the girls to help me. I shooed them away so they wouldn't hurt themselves.

"Will you please, Boots?" I said. "This is nothing!"
"Like the Vatican steps, right?"
But she didn't say anything more. She just watched.

***

As time passed, I began to notice trouble with my lungs more often. I'm the type of guy who lives with something like this. I do the best I can. But when I found myself unable to do things, I couldn't hide it. I never complained to Boots, but she was watching me, and she noticed.

One day she came home to find me worn out, after supervising construction on one of my buildings. I'd had to climb up to the roof to see what the guys were doing up there, and I almost didn't make it. I had been taking it easy all afternoon. I hid my blue fingertips from her as she greeted me, but I couldn't hide the tip of my nose.

I had another bad spell during a visit from Augie. We'd had lunch outside, on the patio, and afterward we were talking about a Frank Sinatra special that had been on TV recently. Gene Kelly had been a guest. The two of them did a dance number, and the way they danced, you'd think they would never stop.

"Augie, how do they do it?" I said. "How the hell—look at them, they're in their sixties, and look at the way they dance. How do they bounce around like that, at their age?"

"What are you talking about?" Augie yelled. "It's nothing!"

He got right up out of his chair and started jumping around, like a kid. If I was 56, he had to be at least 60.

"Augie, what are you, nuts?"

He shook his ass at me.

I laughed so hard, it made me cough until my nose turned blue. Boots noticed. I saw the way she looked at me.

She started to keep a list in her head of all the times she saw me cough or sit down to rest—every time I had trouble breathing.

The last straw came in the summer of 1988, a few months before I turned 60. We were with some friends, a doctor and his wife, on our boat. I had always wanted a boat, but I found out you have to be careful what you wish for. I couldn't go out on the boat alone. The bridge was high up, so when I docked, I needed someone else on board to tie the lines while I steered. That would have been fine, if any of the people who came out with me were ready to help. But whenever I wanted to go out, I had to worry about everyone else's schedule as well as my own, and then I had to pilot while they fished and had a good time. I felt like a tour operator. The worst part was that after we docked, even if they helped me tie up, they would take off. The boat needed to be washed down with a hose, to remove the salt. It should have been a nothing job, but it was a big one for me. Those bastards, they would all leave. "I gotta go! I gotta run!"

This time, we were letting the boat drift, while we had lunch. The motor was still on, but we were in low gear, on open water, in the middle of the Long Island Sound. I came down from the bridge for a few minutes to enjoy myself. Why not? I had a few of the rice crackers that Boots always remembered to bring, along with some cheese and salami she'd picked up on Arthur Avenue. I'd have liked to have a little wine, and to socialize with our guests, but I had to keep an eye on the water too.

Out of nowhere, I saw a floating log very close by. We were headed straight toward it.

"Oooh, *Madonn'*!" I said, and I ran up the ladder to the bridge, to steer around it. I went all in one burst, from the rear deck up to the bridge.

We got around the log with no problem, but afterwards I couldn't breathe. Boots said afterwards that I went white. I had to gasp hard to get air. Everything sucked in, my cheeks, my neck, the skin between my ribs.

"Oh, my God," Boots said.

Her friend, the doctor, just looked at her. Neither of them said anything.

Then Boots got me sitting down again on the rear deck, and she steered us home. She piloted the boat into the dock, and got me upstairs to rest. When I asked, she said our friends were washing the boat. I think she said it just to make me feel good. I slept for a long time afterwards, feeling like I'd been digging ditches all day.

Boots soon had me seeing a pulmonologist, a real *stroonz*. In English, the expression would be that he was full of shit, but the Italian is better: a *stroonz* is a real long piece of shit. He was a little round guy, smooth-skinned, who always wore the fanciest suits. Boots loved that.

I couldn't see how he was helping me. I would go to his office, and he would make me breathe through a tube, an inhaler, to measure my pulmonary function. "You have bullous emphysema," he said, every time. "Your lung function is impaired." He would give me a new inhaler every visit, saying, "Try this." One or two of these medications knocked me out so I could barely make it to my office, but none of them made it any easier for me to breathe. Every time I saw him, he had nothing new to say.

Boots said it was important to let him keep a record of my progress. But it was Boots, not the *stroonz*, who helped me understand what was happening. The injured parts of my lungs had become like balloons, filling slowly with air that could not escape, and all that dead, collected air was pressing against the healthy lungs, keeping me from breathing properly. They called the balloons by a fancy Latin name: bullae. Boots said I had to keep seeing the pulmonologist because the bullae were getting bigger. I could feel what was happening. It might take years, but Boots and the *stroonz* expected that the bullae would eventually suffocate me.

It was hard, really hard, to live with bad lungs. I couldn't climb a flight of steps. I had to leave parties and other social gatherings, because of all the perfume in the room. I couldn't go anywhere that didn't have air conditioning in the summer, when the humidity thickened the air. I couldn't go swimming. When the water hit me, it felt like a punch in the chest. Forget about cutting the grass, or working around the house with things like insulation or sawdust. I could smell a cigarette through my closed car window, if the driver in front of me at a stoplight was smoking. I couldn't even go out to eat on a weekend, or anytime the restaurants were busy, because I couldn't get far enough from the cigarettes.

Donna Lee and Delia were both in college by this time, in 1990. The house felt empty with them gone, but Boots and I were proud of their achievements. At least they were close by, Donna Lee in Providence, Rhode Island, and Delia in Brooklyn. Boots and I took them out sometimes for fancy dinners, so they could feel like our babies again. They didn't say so, but I know that they loved it. Anytime we offered, they never said no.

In the summer of 1990, I got sick with a cold that worsened quickly. The cough wouldn't go away. After visiting the pulmonologist, Boots said my oxygenation was in the 70s. Normal is up above 90. What the numbers meant to me was that breathing had become very hard work. I could hardly get up in the morning, and anytime I sat down during the day, I fell asleep. Boots and the *stroonz* put me on an oxygen tank that I had to carry around everywhere. I asked when I could get off of it, and they couldn't give me an answer.

I started out doing what I had always done. I lived with it. I got up in the morning, went to the office with my little oxygen tank, went through the motions of caring for my buildings and listening to the tenants, returned home, and lay down in bed, with my bigger oxygen tank beside me, for the rest of the day, just trying to breathe.

This is what my father meant when he used to say, *"La vecchiai' è 'na carogna, ma che non'arrivat', è 'na vergogna."* Old age is rotten, but if you don't reach it, it's a shame. I wondered how long this would last. I wanted to get old with my wife, to see my children become women and have their own families. I wondered whether Boots and I would ever travel together to Italy again.

Worst of all were the attitudes I had to face, like that of the building inspector who gave the final approval on my building in Nanuet. I had to sit in my car and wait for the certificate while he did the inspection. The work was almost done, and it was nothing out of the ordinary. It was just a matter of completing a form. He was on the roof, where some men were finishing up.

The inspector yelled down to me, "Miele, come take a look at this."

"I can't," I said. I hoped he could hear me. "I can't make it up there."

He got tough. I was supposed to listen to him, right? He was the one with all the power. "Look, you've got to get up here. I'm going to stop the job if this isn't taken care of."

"I can't."

"What?"

"I can't!" I called, as loudly as I could. It made me cough.

What he did, I could never understand or forgive him for. He stopped the job. Told the men to stop working, the bastard, because, due to my "noncompliance," he had decided to refuse the approval.

I got to a phone somehow, hard as it was for me, and I called his supervisor, who came over right away. All the supervisor had to do was take one look at me, and he told the men, "Finish the job."

Idiots like that inspector hurt me a lot. Those are the people that make it hard for a sick person to keep fighting.

Even with the oxygen, I made sure to visit my family, in the Bronx, Yonkers, and Bronxville. Everyone was in trouble, it seemed.

Augie had cancer of the colon, and was in the hospital more than out. He never stopped with the jokes, weak though he was from the chemotherapy.

I was able to take him to lunch one time, and to a nice place, at that. Augie asked the hostess, a well-dressed and dignified woman, where the restroom was, and she gladly directed him.

When he came back, he said to her, "Madam, I'm afraid that although I used your restroom, I'm still tired."

I was embarrassed, but this woman burst out laughing, and never stopped the entire time we were eating our meal, thanks to Augie's jokes.

Within two months, Augie was gone. I returned to the restaurant, without really thinking about it, at least once more after his death. The same hostess was there, and as soon as she saw me, she started to laugh, and asked about my brother. She didn't even know Augie, but when I told her he'd passed away, she cried real tears.

As for Frankie, his bladder had been removed, also due to cancer. He had to keep himself attached to a little bag that he tucked inside his clothes. For a long time, he hung out on Arthur Avenue, just like always. I would find him there when I drove up to the Bronx to check on him.

I usually pulled over to the curb, so he could get in the car. One time, he got in with a bandage across his hand. "Frank, what did you do?" I asked him.

"Ah, it's nothing," he told me. "One of those punks from the corner tried to tell me off, so I had to teach him a lesson."

I heard later from the other guys that the "punk" was about 40 years younger than Frankie, and about a foot taller. His size didn't save him from Frankie's right hook to the jaw. I always said he could fight bigger guys with no problem, because he had long arms.

The worst was what was happening with Catherine. She had no health problems herself (and neither did Jimmy, that stinker), but she was in the worst shape. Her second son, Billy, was dying of cancer. Us older ones were experiencing what we always knew God had in store for us: the eventual failure of our bodies. Even in our suffering, though, we thanked God that we were not going through the death of a child.

In the spring of 1991, Boots and I started discussing the possibility of surgery to remove the bullae. I was all for it, no matter the risk. My lungs had gotten so bad that I was in bed nearly all day and all night, with the oxygen tube in my nose, just working to breathe. I had a handicapped license plate, so that I only had to walk from the curb to the door of a store when I went out, but even that was too much.

When we visited the *stroonz*, he told us that under no circumstance should I have the surgery.

I said, "Why?"

I wanted to shout at him, to say, what are you, nuts? You want me to die? But my voice was not strong. I couldn't get enough air behind it.

"Armand, your lung reserve is barely anything," he said. "Your oxygenation is far below the normal range. The surgery is too great a risk."

"What risk?" I whispered. I wanted to say, to keep me from dying, you're going to kill me.

Boots spoke up, surprising me. What a look she gave him. "Doctor," she said, "What risk does it pose? If he doesn't have the surgery—we're looking at a very limited life expectancy, perhaps months. If the surgery is successful, he's sixty-two now, relatively young, he can live for many more years in good health. Shouldn't we consider that when weighing the risk?"

The *stroonz* got a little tough. He didn't like being challenged. "You're an anesthesiologist," he said to Boots, as if he were scolding her. "Would you give anesthesia to someone with this kind of lung function?"

Boots didn't back down. "You know," she said, "If it was a gall bladder, or some routine operation, of course I'd be very apprehensive to give this man anesthesia. But this is almost like an emergency, a life-saving procedure, and the impaired lung is the lesion. We're going straight to the defect."

I would have liked to finish the sentence for her, you idiot, but I kept quiet. I was so excited by her speech, so proud of her, that for a second my chest actually felt lighter. I enjoyed watching the *stroonz* try to recover from being made a fool.

A month later, I went into surgery. Boots told me afterward that when the surgeon opened my chest, the bullae were so huge that they rose up out of me like balloons, the size of grapefruits. They had taken up so much room that they had pushed other organs into the wrong places. My heart, for one thing, had turned too far left. The blood vessels around it were getting twisted. When the surgeon moved the bullae, my heart flipped right back into place—boop!—just like that.

"The effect on your oxygenation was immediate," Boots told me later. "The bullae popped out of the chest cavity, and the machine measuring your blood oxygen leaped from seventy-two to ninety-five instantaneously."

As for me—when I woke in the recovery room, from the most beautiful sleep, I couldn't think why I felt so good, until it hit me: I could breathe.

"I can breathe!" I said. It came out louder than I meant it to. I drew a big breath in, and I started to laugh like a madman. "I can breathe!"

I sat up in the bed. I would have gotten right up, but there were tubes attached to my face, and a tugging on my side that stopped me. A nurse was immediately there, telling me to lie back down. I didn't want to lie back down right away. I had been lying down for too long.

"You don't understand, I can breathe," I told her.

"I understand, Mr. Miele," she said. She was friendly and gentle, but strong. She talked to me as she helped me down. "Look! You have a tube coming out of your ribcage that's attached to this machine here. If you try to get out of bed you're going to rip yourself in two."

She showed me the machine that read my blood oxygen level. The number that was 72 before the operation was now 95. As I watched, it climbed to 98.

"See how well you're doing?" she said. "Why don't you try to keep that at ninety-eight, and I'll go get your wife."

I kept repeating, "I can breathe." I said it to myself, though, in between lungfuls of air.

I watched the blue digital number 98 with tears streaming down my face. I thought about my brothers. We never spoke in detail about it, but we had all figured we were dying together. Augie was gone already, the oldest brother and our leader. Frankie might not be long behind. He had stopped hanging out on the corner. My nephew Billy, too, was on his deathbed, while

I was in the recovery room. I had survived again, but it was a bittersweet moment.

***

In the summer, Frankie passed away. That was two brothers I'd lost in less than a year, and I felt it badly. Next to Boots, Frank was my best friend. With his death, my family was more than half gone. Only Catherine, Jimmy, and I were left.

Afterward, all I could talk about was traveling again, to be with our girls. Our young women, I should say. Our daughters had both decided to switch to different schools for their final years of college, schools out west. Out west! How could they leave us all alone?

Here I was, feeling physically better than I had in 20 or maybe even 30 years, maybe better than I'd felt my whole life, yet also more sad and lonely than I'd been in a long, long time. What is the old expression? If Mohammed won't come to the mountain, let the mountain go to Mohammed? Boots and I missed our children, dammit, and we decided that as soon as I was well enough to travel, we were going to follow them out west to remind them how important it was to have family. Nearby.

At least they had gone together. Donna Lee had come up with the idea of going to medical school in Albuquerque, New Mexico, at the state university — who the hell knows why. I think she wanted to go someplace where she could pay her own way. She was at that age when she wanted to prove herself. Delia just wanted to get out of Brooklyn. For that, I didn't blame her. Pratt was in a terrible neighborhood, at the time. But why San Francisco? It was so far away! Anyway, they had driven together, and Donna Lee helped Delia get an apartment in San Francisco before settling herself in Albuquerque. They were lucky to have each other. What the draft and the War did to us brothers — it was disgusting. Pulling us apart when we were so young. My Donna Lee and my Delia, at least, were together.

In October of 1991, Donna Lee met us at the Albuquerque airport. She proudly drove us to the hotel where she'd made our reservation. It had to be the fanciest place in Albuquerque, taller than anything around it. I was suspicious during the days of our visit, waiting for a boyfriend to show up, but she always met us alone. She had planned meals for us at different restaurants. We took a trip to Santa Fe. Donna Lee was worried about taking me to where the air was too thin, but I was fine.

The last night, we went to a Mexican place. Donna Lee had taken us out to many different restaurants, knowing I didn't care for Mexican food, but Boots said, "This is my vacation too! How can we go to Albuquerque and not eat Mexican food?"

We had a wonderful time. We were to take Donna Lee's van the next morning, and drive out to San Francisco to see Delia. I was really looking forward to it, the Painted Desert, the Grand Canyon, the Pacific Ocean. Boots and I were going to make a real trip of it.

We drank a final toast, and I told Donna Lee, "I'm glad you're happy here. But don't forget to come home, eh?"

She gave me a big hug and a kiss, and told me she'd never forget. Boots had tears in her eyes. We'd had Margaritas, and we'd been drinking beer. No Mexican wine, I guess.

We dropped off Donna Lee at her place and drove the van back to the hotel, intending to go to bed and make an early start in the morning. The van was already full of gas. I planned our trip in my head as I started to relax in the bed. Should we take the time to go to Santa Fe again? Or should we stick to the original plans we had for Arizona and San Diego?

The television and the lights were still on, but I was dozing, when the telephone rang. Boots answered it. It was Donna Lee.

"Where are you? Wait—I have to get your father out of bed." Boots held her hand over the mouthpiece and said to me, "Donna Lee is downstairs. She says she has someone with her, and she wants to come up."

"What, a friend?" I said. I'd known this was coming. It had to be the boyfriend. *A'va'Napoli.* "I'm sleeping!"

"Armand, she really wants to come up."

"All right, I'm up!"

I pulled on the shirt and slacks I had set out for the morning. I watched TV while we waited for the knock on the door.

I heard the knock on the door. "It's about time!" I called.

I didn't hear any reply. I moved toward the door, expecting to see some *stonad'* standing there holding my daughter's hand. Boots got there first and opened the door. Then I saw Donna Lee with a terrible look on her face. Standing with her was an old man. A priest.

"Mr. Miele," he said, approaching me. My wife and my daughter were holding onto each other, not saying anything. "I'm very sorry. Your daughter Delia passed away early this morning in California."

I had to sit down. It was as if someone pushed me into the chair. The priest was talking about a car accident early in the morning. The authorities had spent all day trying to find us before they got Donna Lee's address. They had sent a priest because they had found out we were Catholic. This was how they did these things in Albuquerque. How they did it in New York, I had no idea.

I tried to tell Donna Lee, "This is what I've been wanting to tell you kids, that you're all lost, lost without the family." But I could barely whisper.

I began to weep for my youngest daughter. I heaved a big breath as I sobbed, and I remembered that a few months before I couldn't have taken in that much air. I was shaking all over. My throat was tight and my legs still felt weak. But my breathing was fine.

How do you talk about the death of your own child? There are no words. I wanted to die myself, that's the only way to describe it. I wanted to die, if that would let me see my Delia, my brothers, my parents, my nephew. But I had to live, for my wife and for my Donna Lee. And they had to live for me. That's the only thing that kept us all going. We had each other.

***

In making the funeral arrangements, Boots and I decided to build a mausoleum for Delia. We bought double the minimum space for a mausoleum, at St. Anthony's in Nanuet. We had the resources to make a beautiful monument. It helped a little, the idea of making a special place for Delia.

But this was October, and there was only so much that could be done before spring. We looked at granite samples, we looked at drawings by a designer, we thought of statues and plants and stained glass windows, but we couldn't start work on any of it. Delia's casket went into a rough wooden building on the church grounds. No one else was building a mausoleum, so she was the only one in there. The rest of the place was used to store landscaping machinery, old flowerpots, and garden tools. When Donna Lee visited her sister there for the first time, she called it "the Tool Shed", making Boots laugh in spite of everything. It did look funny in a way, the silver casket on the unfinished wood shelves with all the tools, and my wife in her Ferragamo shoes, standing in the dirt every day, twice or three times a day, no matter the weather. On the coldest days that winter she even wore mink earmuffs. The only light was from outside, coming in through the open door and a few cracks in the walls.

Those first few months I felt like I was sleepwalking. I don't know how I functioned. I know that I spent several hours a day at my office, but I don't know what I did there. The place that I most wanted to be was the cemetery, standing in the Tool Shed or walking around our mausoleum plot. Boots and I were glad to have each other for comfort, but we didn't speak much. Donna Lee moved back East to continue school. Boots and I would have loved her to live at home, but we knew we couldn't do much for her. She came home on weekends, often bringing friends along for the ride. They didn't want her to drive alone. That at least made me glad.

Sometime in early December of 1991, Boots was on the phone with Donna Lee, talking about plans for the weekend. I was half-watching the TV. I listened to Boots on the phone. They talked about my birthday (who needs it, I thought) and

Christmas (forget about it), and Boots started to get teary, talking about Delia. Donna Lee said something that got her laughing.

"She had a temper, all right," Boots said. "But there was no one, no one sweeter when she felt like it. Living with Delia was really the agony and the ecstasy!"

She laughed again, and then she cried some more, leaving me to think about "The Agony and the Ecstasy".

"The Agony and the Ecstasy" was a biography of Michelangelo, one of the few books I had ever read for pleasure. I could never understand how people read books that were just made-up stories or poetry, in which someone might write for pages about the color of a tree. Someone who wrote a book like "The Agony and the Ecstasy", though, had to base everything on research. That guy really had to write the truth. I remembered the story of Michelangelo journeying all the way from Rome to Carrara to get marble for a sculpture, because nowhere else was there stone that white. Everyone told him the marble could not be quarried, that there was no way to transport it down the face of the mountain. But he managed it. All those years ago, with no trucks, no diesel cranes, no power tools, just man-power and know-how, he began quarrying for marble in Carrara. To this day, the best marble in the world is quarried there.

"That was something, 'The Agony and the Ecstasy'," I said to Boots, when she got off the phone. "We should go to Carrara."

"Sure, let's get a statue for the mausoleum," she said.

"The sculptors there, they'll make anything you want."

We both looked at the TV for a moment, not saying anything. Boots started to cry again. I knew she was thinking the same thing I was. We were both wondering whether any sculptor could capture Delia in white Carrara marble.

"That will be some trip," I said, getting teary myself, "to the marble quarries in Carrara. Do you think Donna Lee will come?"

This helped us cope. With the addition of the statue, our plans were complete.

***

With our oldest daughter accompanying us, we made the trip to Italy in January, right after New Year's of 1992, bringing photographs of Delia to show the sculptors of Carrara. Everywhere we turned, there was a studio right on the street, packed with beautiful white sculptures of all kinds. We shook hands with the man who was most respectful of our grief, whose sculptures were the most realistic and graceful. He even showed us the rough marble he would use. He put our photographs up on an easel in his studio, and asked us to return in two months.

When Boots and I realized we would be traveling back and forth to Italy more than once to see the progress of the statue, we almost felt light-hearted.

The mausoleum was finished in the spring. It was built to be a monument, not just a grave, and we tend it to this day. I hope our family will care for it far into the future. A slate walkway leads toward the surrounding rose-colored granite wall, which is carved into the shape of an arched gateway. On the arch is engraved a picture of a girl seen from behind, walking through a garden gate. She is surrounded by flowers, birds, and animals. When you walk around to the other side of the wall, where the mausoleum is, you see the same girl from the front. It's Delia. The animals around her are all the family pets that died before her. Some of Delia's artwork is engraved along the inside of the wall, along with the names of my parents, my wife's parents, and all our loved ones who have passed away. The inscription inside the wall reads, "We, the living, keep their memories alive."

The mausoleum itself is of the same rose-colored granite, with an arched face to match the arched-gateway shape of the wall. Inside, on the vault, is engraved a poem written by Donna Lee. Outside, in a patio and garden area, there are four granite benches, engraved with poetry written by my wife's sister, an English professor.

It was really therapy for me, building the mausoleum, therapy that I could understand. I'm not cut out for the usual sitting and talking. Boots didn't feel comfortable with that either, but she had her own form of therapy. She went to church every day. She said her rosary, as she had when we lost Robert. She built up a stack of books beside the bed that got to be waist-high, books by people who brought comfort to the living by talking about — and to — the dead.

The books weren't helpful to me. Why should I read a book about someone talking to dead people? I went to the cemetery every day, sat by the mausoleum, and spoke to the dead whenever I wanted to. I didn't need to hear them answer to know they were there. Why should I go to church? When I visited the mausoleum to sit with my daughter and my parents, I knew that God was there too. I didn't need a priest to tell me that.

I am a man of action. Boots reads; others talk. Building the mausoleum made me realize that the act of creating something useful or helpful was the one thing that helped my pain. In the years following my daughter's death, I think this is what saved me and kept me going. What brought back my spirit was the call to action.

Top Left: Speaking
out about the Spring
Valley Toll, 1996

Above: My "official"
thank-you from the
Ramapo Republican
Committee

Left: Me with
General Petraeus,
2009

A Ripe Old Age

Party Politics and the News

I was from the ghetto. I had always thought that a man making a good living, with a home, with family and friends, and with time to enjoy it all, had made it.

But God had other plans for me.

I didn't expect to survive the loss of my Delia Grace. The pain tore my heart out; parents will understand the feeling. But through my family's support, I did survive it. And because I still had a life to live, I looked for work to do. But what kind of work, I would never have predicted. The spark to carry on came, as always, from my family.

In 1994, three years after Delia's death, my Donna Lee and her husband Ken had our first grandchild, Armand Paul, named after me and Ken's father. Donna Lee and Ken were not living in New York at the time, but they came to visit frequently. There can be no mourning in a house where there is a grandchild. The light that the baby brought, whenever he came to our home, kept us going and kept us strong.

Donna and Ken would go on to have four more boys over the next ten years, and not only that, but in 1996 they moved right next door to us, so that we saw those children every day. They reminded me of my childhood with my own brothers, and all the fun we used to have. Watching my daughter, with the minivan, the washing machine, the dishwasher and the vacuum, I wondered how my mother had done it all by hand. But those children brought back life to our family.

When I looked at my grandchildren, I naturally began to think about how to help provide something for their future. Financially, I had already done all I could. I began to look around me at our community, our town, and our county, and to notice ways in which I could give something to the younger generations, as an older person with a wealth of experiences to share.

One thing I could never stand was the inappropriate use of government power, because of my experiences with people from building inspectors and planning boards, to the policemen who bullied shoeshine boys. To me, one of the worst examples of unfairness in Rockland was the Spring Valley toll. It became a natural target for my anger, as I began to recover from grief.

***

It was impossible at that time to use the Thruway to cross Rockland without paying the toll, and as a real estate broker I crossed the county many times each day. The Thruway Authority was collecting most of those tolls from Rockland residents like me. Not only was waiting in line during rush hour to pay the toll for a 10-minute trip a nuisance, but I was convinced, it was also a health hazard. All those cars and trucks idling on the toll lines were polluting the local air.

Over the years, the toll went from 10 cents, to 15 cents, to a quarter. In the 1990s it finally went up to 40 cents. You had to dig for all that change every day, usually more than twice. I paid that toll for over 20 years.

In 1993, the New York State Thruway Authority introduced the E-Z Pass system. No more coins. Just end-of-the-month bills. Totaling the bills, I realized that toll was costing me over $1000 a year. To me that was another sizable tax on the people here in Rockland County, and it wasn't fair. That's how I got into politics.

In 1995, I attended the Ramapo Republican Convention with the toll in mind, but the party was nominating candidates to run for Town office.

The nominating committee said they were not going to put up a candidate against Town Supervisor Herb Reisman, and I got excited. Reisman had been in office for almost 10 years, never opposed. The politicians seemed happy with this, but not the people. Taxes were always going up, and there seemed to be no accountability. And what were the increased taxes doing for us? In all the time Reisman had been in office, the only things people credited him with were bringing in the sewers and improving some roads. If those were the only improvements he'd brought, why were the taxes going up every year? I stood up at the meeting, and demanded to know why the party wasn't nominating someone to run against Reisman.

The committee put me off. They didn't want to run anyone against him. My inquiry caused a commotion. I insisted we should nominate a Republican candidate. As the noise and gavel slamming was going on, someone from the floor called out, "I nominate Miele!" I was sure it was a joke, but someone else seconded the nomination, and then everyone on the floor was yelling that they wanted me to run.

I went home that night as the Republican nominee for the office of Ramapo town supervisor.

I had held the nomination for less than 12 hours when I turned the radio on the next morning, as I always did, to hear the news, and that's how I heard that the party had decided to strip me of the nomination. "He's not a member of the Republican party, so he cannot by our rules be nominated to run for office on our party's ticket."

The people had spoken the night before; they wanted me to run. And instead of helping me, the Republican leaders were standing in my way. The issue could easily be resolved by a form called a "Wilson Pakula," mandated by New York law, which allows a party chairman to sign for the candidacy of an unregistered nominee. And the chairman wouldn't sign it.

Well, I thought, this was America, not a monarchy, and it was anti-democratic for the party to override the will of the people just like that. Politics like this could kill democracy.

I went to the party offices, to the Board of Elections, to judges, and I found out that if I could prove that a certain number of registered Republicans wanted me, I could force a primary. I had to collect 500 signatures, and the Board of

Elections had to confirm that every single signature was from a legitimate, registered Republican.

It was a mighty struggle. After collecting more than 1000 signatures of registered Republicans, I was able to force the primary. My potential voters had to hand-write votes for me, because I was not officially on the Republican ticket. Three Republican mayors actually endorsed the Democrat, Herb Reisman, in the midst of this!

Nevertheless, I won the primary and got on the ballot as a Republican candidate for town supervisor. I had made the Spring Valley toll a big part of my platform, along with government accountability to taxpayers, and wasteful tax-and-spend government in general. My opposition had picked on me for my position on the toll, for insisting that the town supervisor could do anything about the Thruway Authority's unjust treatment of Rockland drivers. I was called a loose cannon, a political gadfly, and a lot of other things, no doubt. A nuisance, in other words, and not a serious person. But when the people spoke, I won the candidacy.

And after I won the primary, Reisman, one of the inside guys, a "serious" politician, was shaken up enough that he actually came out against the Spring Valley toll himself! Nobody told him he was crazy. Nobody told him that the supervisor had no power to get rid of the toll. Just by forcing a primary, I had made the Spring Valley toll an issue that people were willing to discuss at last.

On Election Day, it rained like mad. We bussed people to the polls who couldn't get there on their own; we earned something like a third of the votes. It was a good number for a local election, especially with the weather, but of course I lost.

Herb Reisman held the office of town supervisor until he died in 2000, still in office, like a king. His successor, Christopher St. Lawrence, was appointed, not elected, and holds the office to this day.

The Spring Valley toll, though, was now at the front of everyone's mind. Also, while a handful of Ramapo Republicans had not endorsed me, I had earned the respect of the

Republican leaders of Rockland County. They approached me to ask if I'd run on the ticket for state assembly.

***

George Pataki, a Republican, had just been elected governor, and the state senate had a Republican majority. The Republicans thought the time was ripe to get a Republican majority in the assembly too. So they asked me to run, because they knew it would be a fight to get a seat away from the incumbent, Sam Colman, and they knew I could fight because of how I ran against Reisman and challenged the Ramapo Republicans.

Now, the state Republicans had grumbled that it was the Democratic governor and the Democratic assembly who would not get rid of the Spring Valley toll. I thought, now that we had a Republican governor, we'd get it done, because he'd support the senate majority. And so, at a Republican fundraiser, I made it known that getting rid of the Spring Valley toll remained among my top priorities. Assemblyman Joe Holland said to me, "You're pissing into the wind." I almost fell to my knees. I couldn't believe it. This was one of our most important local Republicans, who had been using the toll in his own campaign, saying it was unjust for Rocklanders.

Every day as I paid that toll, sometimes even four times a day, I passed a little blue sign that read, "Eisenhower Interstate System." But the sign on the toll read, "New York State Thruway Authority." Why should the money collected on a federal road be going to a state office? What if the Spring Valley toll was actually illegal?

I went to the archives in Albany, and looked at all the laws. I was right. This was not a legal toll. Interstate 87/287, passing through Rockland to the Hudson River, was part of the Eisenhower Interstate System. When the Interstate was built, 90 percent of the costs to run it were supposed to be paid by the U.S. government, and 10 percent by the states. The only tolls allowed were pre-existing, state-run tolls, where the Interstate incorporated parts of older, state-built highways. There was originally a toll in

Hillburn, on a state highway, but the Thruway Authority moved it to Spring Valley after the Interstate had been built. It was not currently on a portion of road originally built by the state. It was a state toll on a federal highway, an unauthorized toll.

I had to prove it. So I went back to the people who supported me when I ran for supervisor, and we got 1000 signatures protesting the toll. I brought my research and all those signatures to the Rockland County Legislature, and told them the toll was illegal. Would they sign a petition to get the issue onto the governor's desk?

The legislators couldn't wait to sign my petition, now that I was a Republican candidate for state office.

There was one person who did not sign: Rockland County Executive Scott Vanderhoef. At the time I couldn't understand why. He was a Republican, and as I said before, the Republicans had been campaigning against the toll for years. It wasn't long before I found out why: the same old story, politics.

It was a matter of some $8.5 billion that former Governor Mario Cuomo, Pataki's predecessor, had borrowed to balance the State budget. How did he plan to pay that money back? Thruway tolls.

Cuomo had ignored the fact that the tolls were in place strictly to pay off the Thruway's construction bonds. The bonds were to mature in 1996, at which time there were to be no more tolls. This put the Democrats in a bind. As the time to remove the tolls approached, the Democratic assembly balked, because they didn't want a Democratic governor to be stuck with $8.5 billion in debt. The Republican senate wanted to remove the toll. But with a Republican governor the positions were reversed. Now the Democrats wanted the toll removed, and the Republicans wanted it to continue! So the toll became just another election issue between the parties.

And me, I was in between, where I found out how hard it was to get things done if you belonged to a party. You get things done when the party has no power over you. That's how it works.

In this confusing political climate, I put my signed petition on Pataki's desk, and showed him my proof about the illegal placement of the Spring Valley toll. To his credit, once all the facts were in front of him, he did not ignore the law. Lo and behold, they removed the toll.

As usual, I didn't get the credit for it. The credit went to County Executive Scott Vanderhoef, who hadn't even signed my petition. As the head of the Rockland Republican Party, he got the credit. He didn't even know the facts. But regardless, we got the toll removed.

I was extremely thankful when I lost the state assembly election. I was done with running for office. It seemed that a politician had to do a lot of talking, without getting anything done.

***

County Legislator Sanford Rubenstein, for instance, was working to establish the first no-smoking law in Rockland. I was very eager to see this law ratified, after barely winning my personal battle to breathe in 1991. Again, because of politics, because of concerns about which party had ownership of the bill, the committee in charge wouldn't let the issue come up for a vote in the full legislature. So I approached Rubenstein and I said to him, "Hey, guess what. I think you're right, and I'm going to get that bill out there."

He said, "You know what, Miele, if you could get the Thruway toll out, I'm sure you can get this bill through."

"I will."

I knew I was in a good position to do this is because I was not running in any election. I didn't care who got the credit. I just knew what it was like for people with lung problems. I knew how they suffered.

This was how I ended up in front of the Rockland County Legislature at a publicly attended meeting, with an oxygen tank fixed to my nose, making a speech right alongside local tobacco lobbyists and the county commissioner of health. I didn't need the oxygen tank anymore, but wearing it made an impression, as I talked about my history of lung disease.

Within 30 days, a bill was in place for the vote, and it passed.

***

If nothing else, my time in politics taught me that you get more things done working outside of the parties. And this is what made me interested in getting involved with the Rockland County Times, a prestigious paper founded in 1888.

It was not an easy road, becoming owner and publisher of a paper. I had to weather one editor who tried to undermine me at every turn, and others who were only interested in bleeding our profits dry. To go into all the Byzantine details of the corruption that I faced is more than I can do here.

But after settling that business, I was able to establish the Rockland County Times as a strong, fair voice speaking to a wide range of subscribers in Rockland County and the surrounding areas. The paper became my proudest accomplishment. We took up issues that made a real difference in lives of ordinary people: health, housing, taxes, land use and basic rights, and most of all, local politics.

I now write an op-ed column about these issues. Yes, I'm a columnist, and I think it's the most important thing I've ever done. When I look back on where I came from, it seems unbelievable, an impossibly long journey. I turn back the pages of this book to read about my own childhood, and have a hard time picturing myself as that boy who sold shopping bags to bring pennies home to his mother.

What I've done in Rockland County has gone a long way toward turning grief and despair over my daughter's death into the best work I've done, something with a real, positive impact on people's lives. All my struggles have been rewarded.

How I wish my mother, my father, my brothers—all of them, especially my Delia, were here to see it.

PART TWO

Miele's Musings

ROCKLAND
COUNTY TIMES
ROCKLAND'S OFFICIAL NEWSPAPER SINCE 1888™

| 124th Year | PUBLISHED WEEKLY | 20 PAGES | 75¢ |

Above: Rockland County Times receives award in from Pearl River Park & Activity Committee, 2004

* * * * *

Top Right: My parents celebrate a family occasion, circa 1955

* * * * *

Right: AMA Realty Office Nanuet, NY circa 1978

The "Merd'i'can" Way

Some, in this nation of liberty, abundance, and opportunity, have the type of attitude that made my brothers and me sometimes say "Merd'i'can"*, instead of American. They think that a life of freedom means a life of hedonism. I don't believe that is the America that our founders intended.

Americans today often forget their priorities, or get mixed up between principle and mere whim. First things first! Get your priorities straight. You'll set yourself up for a happy, productive life.

Once, when I was selling real estate in the Bronx, a couple walked into my office. The wife told me that they had just left the home of her husband's co-worker. I was familiar with the lovely home; it was nearby. She said, "He makes the same salary as my husband, and I can't understand how he can have such a beautiful home while we're living in a three-room apartment." Maybe she was thinking that her husband was keeping money from her, or that the co-worker was a Mafioso or a crook. She was wondering, Why can't I spend more money?

After asking her a few questions, I said one word to her: "Priorities."

Their friend, the homeowner, knew how to prioritize in order to make ends meet. He was making mortgage payments on his home and he worked to protect his investment. He stayed home on weekends, mowed his own lawn, and made his own repairs.

"Madam," I said, "From what you've told me, your priorities, I'm sorry to say, are vacations every chance you have,

---

* My brothers and I used to say the phrase meant "dirty dog"; the ruder translation is "dog shit." I hope that it serves to remind us that Americans can either live up to the promise of our liberty, or be made rotten by it.

trading your car in for a new one every few years, and treating yourself to restaurants frequently, with no thought of the added expense. You are only thinking of the good times and have no concern for how you're hurting your own future."

I don't know what became of that couple, but the homeowner they told me about, like many others, continued to put first things first for many years. Twenty years later, his home was not only still beautiful, but was worth much more than what he could have saved in a bank.

When you mix up your priorities with your whims, you get into trouble, financially and personally. If you say your family is your first priority, plan your time and your finances accordingly. You may have to deny yourself the indulgence of an expensive evening for two and go to a family restaurant instead. If you are single, and your work is your number one priority, you may not have the freedom to plan long vacations or late evenings with friends. Don't let your priorities in life suffer for the sake of spending hours or dollars you can't afford on flat-screen TVs or a weekly golf game.

Take your choice of priorities very seriously. Think long and hard about starting a family, or about pursuing a demanding profession. Don't get discouraged; just understand what you are getting into. The better you understand how to create the life you dream about, the more success and happiness you will enjoy.

What are the American priorities I value? I think that loyalty to family, God, and country is a good place to start. These values are celebrated in the holidays we enjoy as a nation. Strong American values even helped me through the life-threatening experience of cancer. When you know what you have to live for, you fight harder. As you'll see from musings that follow, everything falls into place once you have your priorities straight.

It's Not What You Earn, It's How You Spend

August 21, 2008*

I lived through the Great Depression in the tenements of New York City, one of a family of five children. We were happy. We never felt deprived. Maybe it was because we didn't know anything other than what we had. We had food, shelter, and clothing. We had the warmth and security of family. Nobody told us we needed anything more; we never realized how little we had.

Money was for spending on the necessities. First came the food to fill our stomachs, such as bread, pasta, beans and vegetables. Fruit and dessert were too expensive. We rarely ate meat, and when we did it was mostly liver, which was so cheap that the Americanos fed it to their animals. Sometimes we got the shanks of the lamb, full of tendons, but my mother knew how to prepare it so that it melted in your mouth. We ate fish on Fridays because of the Catholic religion. My mother bought only the cheapest varieties, loaded with bones. Clothing was also the most basic that money could buy, always handed down, with the exception of underwear and what we got from home relief, when my father worked as a stone cutter for the Works Progress Administration (WPA). Rent was least in the walkup apartments, with the higher and rear apartments being the cheapest.

If we learned anything during the Depression, it was that if you had the opportunity, you earned some money. We also learned how to spend wisely. Jobs were scarce. We saved our money, and never bought anything that we could do without. We never bought a new replacement for something that could be repaired.

My father was the breadwinner. The WPA only guaranteed two weeks' work a month, but he found other work as a day

---

* Most recent publication dates are given for Miele's Musings. Many of these columns have been reprinted frequently over the years; see the Introduction.

laborer, to keep us fed, warm, and dry. He and many others also squatted on vacant lots, to plant food for their families. We children all pitched in the best we could. Today some might equate the manual labor we did with child abuse, but I call it a lesson in family values. We were taught to be proud and stand on our own two feet. This is why we were closer to each other than some families are today.

The whole community worked hard just to get a meal. I remember a man building his house, and every day the men from the neighborhood asked him for work. They hung around and helped, working just to be fed. He ended up building his house with almost free labor, but he fed the whole neighborhood for weeks, if not months.

Were our family values any different from others? I don't think so. Every family that has to go through difficult times together experiences the same thing, no matter what nationality, religion, or race. My parents found that in the United States, unlike Italy, with hard work and perseverance, they could give their family a better life. Maybe is why they were never discouraged, when American families in the same financial situation might have lost hope. Americans sometimes forget that the good life is not just for the asking, by virtue of being American. You have to work for it, and you have to save for it.

Unfortunately, so many in the United States today think that crazy spending is part of the American way. Families get into financial trouble listening to the television, radio, newspaper and mailing advertisements that constantly offer great sales and easy credit. I say it's only a sale if you need it, otherwise forget it. We are spoiled — spoiled in the sense that we go into debt for the non-necessities.

Many of the unemployed have been out of work for months, or even more than a year, and blame the recession. But how many have dropped out of the labor force because they couldn't find work to their taste? There are many jobs out there. It's just that people can't earn enough to maintain their bloated lifestyles. Spending wisely is an art. It can put you in the black, and keep you out of the red. Your earnings are a fact that's hard to change; but if you spend wisely, you can change your life for the better.

No one wants to go back to the lifestyle people had to lead during the Great Depression. But the values we adopted should not be forgotten: work hard, make the most of opportunities, live within your means, and if you are lucky enough to have a loving family around you, never forget to put them first.

——

Does Learning Ever End?

July 24, 2010

"No more pencils, no more books, no more teachers' dirty looks!" Remember how we used to happily call this out, when school closed for summer recess?

It's no different for children today. End of the school year! Start of vacation! No homework, no more early-to-bed-early-to-rise, no more rushing to catch the bus. No more nagging from Mom and Dad, "Did you do your homework? Don't forget your books! Be careful! Don't fight!"

But wait—what about the parents' summer vacation? Now you have to plan your children's whole day, starting with breakfast at a different time. The children hang around the house, getting in the way all the time, and now they are the ones doing the nagging! "What is there to do, Mommy? Why this, Mommy, and why not that?"

This is all new to young parents. They may find themselves crying for the first time, and not the last, "When are they going to grow up and do things for themselves?"

But parents, please remember, no matter how busy you are, the time to be concerned for your family is now, when the children are growing. Many times I have heard ambitious people say, "I devoted my life to a purpose and succeeded. I want to devote my later years to my family."

Guess what those people often discover? Once they find the time for their children, their children have already grown up. Not only that, but the children have lost interest in waiting for their parents' "quality time".

Know and watch your children. Don't be a stranger to them. Get involved now, to save the most precious part of your family's life.

Before you know it, your children will have to grow up and do things for themselves, but now they need your guidance. The day comes for the great step forward of graduation from high school, and some of these young adults still think it's "no more pencils, no more books." But now they need most of all to learn that there really is no end to discipline and hard work, if they want to succeed.

They may say, when they leave home for the first time, "Mom! I can take care of myself! I can stay out late! I know when to study! My friends are the best!"

But they still have a lot of growing up to do, and they still need you. I remember my nephew asking to borrow my car once, saying, "What's the problem? I'm nineteen years old, I'm a man!"

But when I scolded him about the car coming back with no gas and low oil, he excused himself. "How would I know? I'm only a kid!"

A parent often dreads the moment of confrontation with a growing teenager. But I say that when misunderstandings crop up, the best thing is to stop and admit, "I am learning just as you are. I never parented a teenager before, so forgive me if I misunderstand. Please try to understand me, and I will do the same for you. Is that a deal?"

I wish all of our new graduates congratulations and lots of luck — but remember that your family gave you your start, and you still need them. Stick with your ideals, and don't be a wannabe. It only brings trouble. Try being yourself; it works! With dedication and hard work, you will succeed.

Parents with children at home, keep them safe this summer. Every year, little ones encounter dangers that could be avoided, and the older children take unnecessary risks. Do what you can to educate your children about how to avoid danger, and never take their safety for granted.

Look out for the dangers in what seems like innocent fun, too. Children are viewing more sex, violence, and illicit behavior on TV, the Internet, and in movies than ever before. Studies by organizations like the National Institutes of Mental Health and the American Academy of Pediatrics agree that the increasingly mature themes in children's entertainment are linked to clinical depression among children.

Don't worry about just keeping busy during the holidays. Spend some time together! Learning does not take place only in school. It never stops.

―――――

Valentine's Day

February 10, 2009

We older folks like to say that youth is wasted on the young. But is it, really? I think that on Valentine's Day, young lovers should look to seniors for assurance that romance gets better with age.

Valentine's Day is what my brother, a boxer, used to call "amateur night". We older partners, who are honest, sincere, and loving family people, can start off Valentine's Day by reminiscing about the good and bad times that brought us to where we are, together. Many of us celebrate with children and grandchildren. The popular attitude is that the elderly no longer appreciate the more romantic thrills of Valentine's Day.

But think about what this holiday means to us older folks. Do we renew our vows? Not necessarily. If you've been with your partner a long time, your vows may never seem old or faded; you already think more than once a year about love! Do we just let Valentine's Day pass by, and say that it's for the young? No way. If anything, we know how to celebrate with elegance. The young have the excitement of pretending to be grown up on Valentine's Day—they certainly have their excitement ahead of them—but we have the thrill of really being grown up, and really being in love!

Do you want to help young people to have a happy Valentine's Day? Show them what it means to be in love! The young imitate the older generations. In the usual day-to-day, they look to parents to provide all the things they have become accustomed to: cash handouts, good food at regular mealtimes, and transportation to school, sports, music lessons, and social events. Think about whether the young people in your life can also look to you to understand a little about being in love!

Have they seen you hold hands, whether in good times or in bad? Do they know that you've come through a lot together? Tell them your stories, and show them how happy you are! You single parents have stories, too. Share them, and let your children know that you haven't given up on love.

But don't sweep love under the rug, or pretend that romance is either all good or all bad. If you have children, they will be teenagers sooner or later, and they'll find out for themselves, anyway.

Teenaged love — that's when your worries as a parent really begin! It's bad enough for parents when teenagers start to think they are grown up. They think they know it all. They think their friends know it all. But when teenagers think they've fallen in love, parents are really in for a hard time, because teenagers think that whoever they're in love with knows more than anyone!

Isn't this the start of many young love stories? Most of them are short and bittersweet. Parents, your own love story will soon include your child's first love and heartbreak. During first romances, young people begin to understand what we've been telling them all along, that love is hard work!

Look to the older generation for the meaning of true romance. They've spent the time, and know what love is about.

For everyone with families, reminiscing about the happy days and the hard times; and for the young amateurs, imagining they are in love; have a happy Valentine's Day. Don't go wild. Just enjoy yourselves and have fun.

———

St. Patrick's Day

March 24, 2011

It's a great day for the Irish. You don't have to be Irish to enjoy the festivities, though. Everyone is welcome to join in, just don't forget the wearing o' the green! The Irish have come a long way in gaining the respect they deserve, having fought side by side with all Americans and raised wonderful families.

The great Irish migration to the U.S. started in the 1850s, when Irish dock workers could earn $1.25 a day in New Orleans. In Ireland, a more typical wage, if they could find work, was 8 cents a day. Even when a plague hit New Orleans, the Irish immigrants did not stop; the boats just changed course, and headed to Boston. They knew that America was the place to be! The Irish found any work that was available to them, no matter how hard, whether in factories, construction sites, coalmines, or elsewhere.

At first, the men came alone, and would send money back to the families left behind in Ireland. This was tough. There was plenty of discrimination against the Irish, and like other immigrants, they suffered poor living conditions. In fact, the close quarters they lived in were probably similar to how the homeless live today, because that was all they could afford. But the families back home in Ireland only got letters saying what a wonderful country this was, and of course how they missed the beautiful Irish women.

Young Irish women then received permission from their parents to leave for America. Their first jobs were as housemaids. The women sent most of their earnings home, just as the men did, but they lived in better conditions, because they worked for the upper class as maids or cooks, instead of doing manual labor. While learning their work in genteel homes, these young women also learned how the upper class lived. Unlike their fellow male immigrants, many Irish women had the opportunity, through their employers, to go to school. As a result, Irish-American women became known as dedicated nurses, or for starting religious schools and orphanages. They eventually inspired great respect among Americans.

Irish-Americans further proved themselves by taking up arms for their adopted country during the Civil War, and later in every armed conflict involving the U.S. We have to be very proud of the great heroes of Irish descent, both living and dead, who risked everything to keep America free.

Many immigrants had similar struggles, coming to the U.S. in the 1800s. They started from the bottom, from less than nothing, and always had a tough hill to climb. The payroll records from the construction of the Kensico Dam back in 1890 explain the situation perfectly. White laborers were paid $1.35 per day, Black laborers $1.35 per day, water boys $1.35 per day, and Italian laborers 10 cents less than anyone else, $1.25 per day, just because they were Italian. They were the lowest of the low, at the time. So when you see today's Italian-American families, who are now part of the mainstream, highly successful in business and politics, you know how hard they had to fight to get there. Once upon a time, the ancestors of Mario Cuomo, Antonin Scalia, and Lee Iacocca were worth less than the water boys on a construction site.

Each year's St. Patrick's Day celebrations remind all descendants of immigrants what their ancestors had to endure. Irish, Italian, Polish, German, Black, Asian, Middle-Eastern, they came from the world over, wanting to be free to practice their religion, to work, and most of all to educate their children and preserve their families' values.

To the legal immigrants of today, you may be starting from the bottom, but you have a head start and a great opportunity thanks to the immigrants that came before you, whose descendants welcome you here. Maybe you can look at celebrating St. Patrick's Day as the start of your new life in the United States.

———

What's "American-Italian"?

October 8, 2009

In New York City, the Columbus Day Parade starts on Fifth Avenue at 44th Street, and runs all the way to 79th Street. This is the largest Columbus Day Parade in America, honoring Christopher Columbus, of course, one of the world's most famed Italians.

On Monday, October 10, 2005, the parade's grand marshall was U.S. Supreme Court Justice Antonin Scalia. Justice Scalia, raised in Queens, New York, was the only child of an Italian immigrant father, professor of Romance languages at Brooklyn College, and his American-born mother, a daughter of Italian immigrants. Justice Scalia climbed a long road to beat the odds against the children of Italian immigrants. He graduated from high school at the top of his class, then proceeded to graduate summa cum laude from Georgetown College and magna cum laude from Harvard Law School. He worked as legal counsel for two U.S. presidents, and taught at the University of Virginia, the University of Chicago, Georgetown University, Stanford University, and Tulane University. Then he became the first American of Italian descent to be appointed a justice of the Supreme Court of the United States.

I say that Justice Scalia and the millions who share his heritage are American Italian, meaning American first. With due respect to his own heritage, any immigrant should consider himself American first. Your heritage is very important; it is your blood, but never forget that your rightful place is here, in the United States. It's only right to honor your American status first.

While I was growing up in the old walk-up tenements of the Bronx, immigrants and their children felt more comfortable in the ghettoes, where the customs and the languages of their homelands were respected. In the Italian ghetto, anyone who spoke Italian was considered Italian. We had black Americans who spoke Italian, and they were Italian to us. Those who only spoke English were considered Americano, or outsiders. It used to be that you left your parents' home only when you got married, and even then, you always lived in the same neighborhood, along with your uncles, aunts, and cousins, and your friends' extended families too. It was like you were married to the neighborhood community, "until death do us part!"

We've come a long way from the close-knit ghetto families. Immigrants served with honor in the great American wars, became successful in business and in academics, and slowly left the neighborhoods, because we didn't need them in the same way anymore. We were American first.

American-Italians are now accepted with pride in mainstream society. We don't have to rely on the neighborhoods for protection and security anymore, but we should continue to honor our ancestors who forged the way for us in the United States. We should strive to be leaders, to new immigrant groups trying to make it here for the first time.

So all Americans and new immigrants should join in and enjoy Columbus Day, because this is an American parade. In this parade, as always, we want to salute the U.S. Armed Forces and our family values. God bless America.

––––––

Mother: the Wonder Woman

May 5, 2011

Ah! Mother's Day. Don't we all wish at times in our lives that we could be babies again, even if for a day, even an hour? Don't we wish we could be held in our mothers' arms? Your mother is always there in your soul, your mind, and your heart. Every day should be Mother's Day. Every day you should honor your mother, or honor her memory.

Here's a story I read years ago. A 96-year-old woman got sick. As she was brought into the hospital, she was moaning, "My baby, my baby."

Her doctor became concerned, wondering whether there was something to this moaning about a baby. He called the police, who went to the woman's little house to find out if there was a child there. That's right: the baby was her 72-year-old son.

Mommies out there, don't laugh! You would do the same. Ask any mommy. No matter what the age of her child, he will always be her baby.

Nowadays, more than ever, we have children growing up with "non-biological" mothers. A woman who becomes a mother through adoption is just like any other. She instinctively sacrifices almost anything to raise her child. Even a live-in nanny can become like a mother to children whose real mothers are rarely home. The mother's instinct is in these women, and they worry about their children, no matter what their age.

Some people never know their biological mothers, unless they go out and find them. Often when an adopted child is growing up, he has no thought about whether his mother is "biologically" his or not. The questions come about when he has his own family. He becomes curious, and would like to have some answers. Why did my mother give me up? Was it because she couldn't take the pressure of having a child? Was it my fault, somehow? Did I do something wrong? Do I have any brothers, sisters, or other blood relatives?

Everyone is happy, at first, when the grown adoptee finds his biological mother, but the process can hold some surprises and disappointments. The adoptee might feel resentful or guilty, and these feelings are confusing. A person who grew up without parents might see how years of not getting held or hugged was a loss for both the parents and the child. Maybe he begins to wonder about his mother's sorrow at never witnessing his childhood pleasures and pains. He begins to understand a little of what it means to be a mother, what his biological mother had to go through for him to come into the world, and what his non-biological mother has been going through to raise him to be who he is.

I have often wondered, does it matter that I wasn't adopted? Is there a difference? I don't believe so. What I know is that my mother, with all of the heartaches and the problems of raising five children during the Depression, had to be a dedicated, loving woman. No washing machine, no dryer, only human dishwashers.

For me, mothers are wonder women. They dedicate their lives to their families, when a child comes along. It's an enormous responsibility. It takes endurance and strength. The mother becomes the link that keeps the family together. Those of us who can only reminisce about our mothers feel that tie the most strongly.

On this Mother's Day, if you are lucky enough to have your mother still with you, go give her a great big hug, and don't forget to do the dishes today!

———

Oh, My Papa!

June 10, 2010

Father's Day is here, and it's about time they give us fathers our one day for the year!

Does this sound familiar?

"Hey Pop, you're the best!" Now Pop worries a little. He thinks, "The best what? Is something up their sleeves?" Be on your guard, Pop! Because the kids know that underneath your macho exterior, you are a pushover.

I like to tell this story, which says something about all of us fathers. In my first office, a retired gentleman who lived nearby would visit and keep me company. I was a single man then, and wouldn't dare question him or argue, because I always respected and listened to my elders. He was, besides, the fatherly type, a man with some wisdom, and I hoped I would learn something. The conversation would always revolve around his family, of which he was so proud.

This man had just bought a brand new Cadillac. That was a very big deal in those days, not like today when it seems that anyone can lease any car they want to. The gentleman said that none of his children would ever drive his new Cadillac. They had their own cars. The Cadillac was strictly his car.

I teased him a little, and said, "I'm sure you would let your son use your car." The son I was referring to was a pre-medical student. The father was immensely proud of the son's achievements.

"No way!" was the father's reply. "He has his own car. It will never happen."

I just laughed to myself. This father wanted to show that he was in charge. Sound familiar? Don't all fathers think they are in charge?

One day, the son stopped in my office. I jokingly mentioned what his father had said regarding the Cadillac. The son said, "Mr. Miele, I will get that Cadillac from my father, and he will be happy about it."

Well, the son got not only the Cadillac from his father, but also got all the money he needed for a night out, and his father even wished him luck. The reason this all happened was that the son told his dad, "I'm going to a dinner dance, and my date is Dr. So-and-so's daughter." Her father was well-known doctor in town.

The moral of this story, as I see it, is that when a child really wants something from his dad, all he has to do ask in the right way. A hard-working father, who so often only has time to worry about paying the bills, will always provide for his child, to show his love. He always reserves his softest spot for his child.

Dads, you all have stories about your children wanting something that sounded fishy. Your children think they can put one over on you. You know what? Dad, you may not let on, but you know it every time, and you often give in anyway. A father's thought is, "How can I let my child down?" You forget to be firm. You let the house rules go with just a ceremonial nod, and then you sit and worry, hoping you will not have to come to the rescue.

As for the children, the time will come when they say, "My father always worried about me and I thought he was old-fashioned. I thought I could put one over on him. But boy, was he right!"

Because of the strong family ties your father instilled in you, you foresee your own children's mistakes, and you want to protect them as your father protected you. Dad is more than just the strong back and mind of the family. He is the provider, in his heart and soul.

Happy Father's Day, and don't forget to pick up the tab at the restaurant, to show Daddy how much you respect him. He really is the best. Don't forget to give him a big hug.

The Fear of Cancer

August 26, 2010

You have worked hard all your life, and taken care of your family to the best of your ability. You have survived many of life's struggles, and thrilled to its joys. Now, a new challenge rises up to meet you: cancer. You wonder whether you could have done something differently, to save yourself and your family from the road ahead.

But cancer is not a disease that respects anyone's lifestyle. It strikes indiscriminately. No one can predict with certainty what lies ahead of you, but you are not beyond hope.

Years ago, the diagnosis of cancer was equal to a death sentence. Today this is just not true. With all the advances being made every day in cancer research, people are living many productive years after diagnosis, often defeating the disease altogether. If anything, a cancer diagnosis is the beginning of realizing how precious life is, for you, your family, and friends.

Men, more than women, do not want to face the fact that they are sick. They tend to be macho, and use excuses or scorn. "What does the doctor know? I feel fine. He just wants me to waste money on crazy pills and bunk." Well, I'll tell you something, the reason men make those remarks is because they are afraid, afraid to join the sick, afraid to become dependent.

You can't be macho. When cancer is discovered, it is up to you to immediately seek treatment. Delaying treatment will only increase your suffering down the road. You must have the courage to face cancer head on, from the first sign. You have to trust your doctor when you get a diagnosis of cancer, and you have let your doctor help you face your fear. If you don't go to your doctor, where will you go?

Let's start with your team. There are many experienced doctors and other professionals who know what you are going through, and fortunately are available to help you. You are going to realize that the doctors and hospital personnel, on whom you come to depend, are the most dedicated and concerned people in the world, people of all races, religions and genders, who are united in one purpose: fighting for you. You will become aware, for the first time in your life, of the millions of people working to find a cure for you.

You've never seen or heard of these unsung heroes, the research scientists in the laboratories looking for a cure, the dedicated hospital workers, doctors, nurses, volunteers, fundraisers, working feverishly to find comfort and a cure for humanity. These people never give up and you shouldn't either.

You need to find courage to face this ugly disease, and then the determination to fight to win. Understand what you must do to help yourself.

Help your doctor by listening and giving all the information he or she needs. Do not refuse any examinations or tests that are suggested by your doctor; this is very important. The worst part about the tests is that you feel your body is being violated, which is really hard to take. But it must be done, and you should try not to complain. The doctor doesn't like seeing you under stress any more than you like going through it. All of the tests and studies you go through are stressful experiences, but knowing what to expect will help. You should cooperate as much as possible without brooding, which doesn't help either you or your medical team.

Someday, cancer will be eradicated. It will be controlled or conquered like polio, smallpox, measles, mumps, diphtheria, tuberculosis, chicken pox, HIV, and many more were. Genetic and microbiological research in recent years has helped to fight viruses and allergies, and is being used to fight cancer.

I refer to cancer as a battle, and it's a difficult battle to face. It's up to you to hang tough. Have courage; do not give up. Don't let your family and all the believers who are praying for you down. A cancer diagnosis is tough to take but if possible, you should focus on the fact that you are not in a hopeless situation. Something can be done to help you. There are many survivors who have defeated cancer more than once. Cancer fears the one who fights the good fight.

Let cancer fear its opponents, and not the other way around.

ROCKLAND
COUNTY TIMES
ROCKLAND'S OFFICIAL NEWSPAPER SINCE 1888™

| 124th Year, No. 23 | PUBLISHED WEEKLY | 20 PAGES | 75¢ |

Above: I interview two elected Rockland County officials in 1999.

Below: Headlines from the Rockland County Times report on waste of taxpayer dollars.

Sherwood says Town Attorney is Paid too Generously

Supervisor-Elect seeks change

BY DYLAN SKRILOFF

to the "Good Old Boys," days of the past.

I was recently re-elected to the Town Board of Stony Point, running on a "sometimes..."

well, but these days are long past. We spent more forward, not backwards. I can attest that this total expenditures for legal services were $355,797 for the year 2005. That's the very bottom line...

Highway Robbery: State Agencies Pilfer Highway & Bridge Funds

list of New York's bad fiscal choices.

New York State's Dedicated Highway and Bridge Trust Fund hasn't been all that dedicated. Since 1991, only 34.9 percent of the money in the fund went directly toward the repair and improvement of the state's deteriorating roads and bridges. And over the next four years, that will shrink to about one fifth. It's supposed to be a "locked box," but apparently the lock wasn't very strong.

The Trust Fund was created in 1991 to fund the construction and rehabilitation of state-owned roads and bridges. But starting in FY 1994-95, the Trust Fund paid debt service for bonds that were issued by the Thruway Authority and never approved by voters. Operational systems and spending were also added to the Trust Fund.

Rockland Taxpayers Fund MTA $28B Spending Plan

Rockland County Exec Proposes Cell Phone Tax

The Unfortunate Taxpayer

We build our lives around strong priorities and family values, but we also want to live in community with other families. There's no question that building a strong community means paying taxes. But too often, those in charge of creating budgets, from the local level on up, forget that the producers of the economy, the taxpayers, should come first.

I write about Rockland County, New York, but I imagine that a lot of Americans' experience with their local taxes is similar to mine. As homeowners, workers, and taxpayers, we build up schools, libraries, roads, parks, villages, town and county buildings, police, and judicial courts. We give our all to our hometowns and counties.

Then we find that because we are homeowners, because we put down roots in these hometowns we have built, local government takes advantage of us by increasing property taxes every year. It begins with some who cry out that we are so fortunate, we should share our wealth. That sounds great, and many of us nobly agree. We made it; why shouldn't we give back to the unfortunate?

Then someone, often involved in local government, creates a program. This requires salaries and an expense account, which increase every year. Eventually the people who created the program either tire of it or chalk up a great success on their resumes, and move out of the county or state, leaving us taxpayers to take care of their program.

Our county's schools, trying to draw young families out of the city with elite programs, create the bulk of the burden, and seniors get hit hardest. In 1972, when I came to Rockland, my school taxes were $1,400. I had two children. By 1988, after they had graduated from the local school system, my taxes were more than double that. In 2010, the school taxes for the same house were $11,000. I had to pay this money or risk losing my home.

A family in my neighborhood experienced this very disaster. Before the foreclosure, the homeowner was going from door to door, begging for help with her school taxes, so that she and her disabled mother would not have to move from their home, which had been in the family for three generations. All the while, the local school district was sitting on taxpayer money, perhaps illegally. In 2010, the New York State Comptroller Thomas DiNapoli determined that hundreds of New York school districts were illegally stockpiling billions of dollars, collected for past budgets and never spent. Who is minding the store, and who is truly unfortunate?

In Rockland, we got hit with a new tax on our cell phones in 2010. We are even taxed by the Metropolitan Transit Authority (MTA). The MTA, mostly concerned with serving New York City, gives Rockland no meaningful say in how our money is spent—isn't this taxation without representation?

I hope that these musings will enlighten readers. Use the vote to keep taxpayers in control of the money for which they work so hard. By capping or reducing taxes, government will allow the middle-income taxpayer to afford the taxes that are already in place. This will help keep the economy going and save many people from losing their homes. Call or write to your elected officials, especially the local ones, if you feel like you're being buried alive.

Who Cares for the Taxpayer?

June 3, 2010

There are two things we cannot beat—death and taxes. The difference between them is that when death comes, we all hope not to suffer; but when it's tax time, there is no hope but to suffer, because paying taxes never ends. Even after you are dead, there are estate taxes to pay.

Working taxpayers know they must pay federal and state tax on the income they earned and worked for. What they do not know is that they are also paying "use taxes," hidden taxes imposed upon them by all levels of government, that are only justified by the fact that taxpayers are using (not necessarily purchasing) the taxed item in New York State. Many times, there is more than one tax on a given article. For instance, you may know that there is a federal excise tax on the price of an automobile. But when a New Yorker buys and registers a new car, state, county, MTA, and other taxes are added on top of the federal excise tax. Replacement tires for your car are also subject to both sales and use taxes. To name all the use taxes is impossible; no one knows how many and what kind of use taxes they are paying for. Even the people who impose them don't keep track.

The politicians nowadays like to say, as an excuse for taxpayer woes, that consumers are spending more than they earn. Who do the politicians think they're kidding? Do they think they're telling us something we don't already know? They should talk about themselves. Government spends more than it takes in all the time, then looks to the taxpayers to fund the "bailouts". Anyone who ran a business that way would go bankrupt. What a way to balance a budget. Watch out! If they tax the water we drink, why not the air we breathe?

Our taxes are high, but they're going to be higher. When Bush was president, the federal budget was up to $600 billion, and people called him all the names in the book. As of 2010, President Obama has us at $1.8 trillion. That right, 1.8 trillion dollars, and it's not over yet.

I've often wondered about the people that impose all of these taxes. Do they think about fiscal responsibility, or even about their families and friends who will be picking up the bill? Do they believe that imposing these taxes doesn't affect them personally, because they can always call for a raise in salary?

All the programs we get taxed for are supposed to make things better for the poor, the sick, the unfortunate and whatever the politicians come up with, but they don't. Look at ACORN, which was supposed to help low-income citizens to have a voice in government, but which became notorious for falsely registering hundreds of thousands of voters, and is now in bankruptcy. In 2008, the New York Times reported a finding by the Association of Certified Fraud Examiners that all organizations, whether government, for-profit or non-profit, lose an average of 6 percent of their revenue every year to fraud, and most of the biggest thieves are the executives leading the organizations. In 2006, the number came to over $40 billion nationwide. I'm not making this up. Check it out yourself: http://www.nytimes.com/2008/03/29/us/29fraud.html.

I believe these programs only improve the lives of the people running them. Nothing changes for the hard-working taxpayer, that's for sure. When the media interviews the man on the street, the reporter always seem to find a person who is in favor of raising taxes. I'd bet anything that guy on the street doesn't know what it is to pay income taxes.

Wake up, America.

———

Government Spends More than Taxpayers Can Afford

February 26, 2009

It would seem like common sense that government budgets should never rise more than the inflation rate in a year. Yet tax increases continually do beat the inflation rate, to make up for the politicians' errors in judgment and to give favors to interest groups. And our leaders have the nerve to tell us taxpayers to never spend more than we can afford!

Local governments are all crying like babies with the typical excuses: it isn't their fault; it's the economy, it's the War, there's not enough federal aid, etc. Since the late 1990s, our local government budgets have been increasing 5 to 10 percent a year if not more, while the inflation rate has been 2.5 percent or less. Let's start with Rockland County schools as an example.

When there was plenty of credit, and the money was pouring in, the schools increased spending on salaries, created new programs, and bought land and buildings to compete with each other. They went wild, thinking the good times would never end. One school district announced that it wanted to get a bond of $187 million, to rebuild 16 school buildings that were 58 years old. What in hell could be wrong with all 16 buildings at one time? There is no concern for the taxpayers, especially the senior citizens and the sick. Many families cannot afford any tax increase, since the parents are already holding two and three jobs. Sometimes they don't even eat properly. They skimp on every necessity: electricity, heat, water, clothes, just to pay the rotten property taxes for fear of losing their homes.

Interest groups get together to lobby for all this spending. To get more money for school programs, the easy way to raise taxes is to claim, "It's for the kids" (they call them baby goats; I prefer to call them children). These groups are planted at local government and school board meetings, and are part of the mess we are in. Parents will give until they bleed, for the sake of their children, and every interest group with a new school program takes advantage of this.

As if over-budgeting were not bad enough, the school boards often find ways to exceed a budget that's already in place. Before putting in a budget, administrators should know how much it costs to run things, shouldn't they? Unfortunately, it doesn't work that way. School boards always go over-budget the sneaky way, using the bond method. They borrow money for new programs or construction, and of course collect the payments due from the taxpayers, but they don't always include new bonds in the same year's budget. New bonds are usually considered separately. The fault occurs when we have to pay off bonds that are not in the budget. This haphazard accounting makes the budgets all screwed up.

Once the budget is in place, the blaming begins. The village blames the town for higher expenses; if it's not the town's fault, then it's the county's; and from the county, the fault goes to the state. Where does the fault stop? It doesn't stop, it goes right to the U.S. government.

In 2009, the federal government used a "stimulus package," a fancy term for printing money we don't have. Printing more money creates inflation. Then the federal taxes go up. The taxpayer has to earn his money to pay bills and taxes; he doesn't have the luxury of being able to print it.

We must stop spending money we don't have. We must make laws about how government is allowed to spend (or is that too old-fashioned?). The first thing to do is to force the government to pay off debt when the money is coming in over the inflation rate. If we start paying off the bond debts, then we will reduce the interest we have to pay. Once the bond debt is being paid down, the "rainy day" or emergency fund should be increased which will in turn increase the interest earnings. The next step is to control new spending. Finally, every four to five years there should be a "give-back" to the taxpayers in the form of new development in parks, transportation, sidewalks, streets, and updating all of the many services; after all, this is what taxes are supposed to do.

For once, elected and school officials, let's have fiscal responsibility! Think of your own family, the taxpayers, the sick, the handicapped, and the senior citizens who have paid their dues to make this a great country. Let's start by having a referendum: the budget increase should never be more than the inflation rate! Such a law would take the pressure off all elected and school officials. We would get rid of every fly-by-night idea-man or organization coming to the government asking for money.

———

Equitable School Taxes

December 10, 2009

Why did a year of education in the Rockland County public schools cost more than $18,000 per student in 2009? Why does this number increase every year? Why did Rockland school taxes increase by 60 percent from 1995 to 2005, while the inflation rate added up to only a 28 percent increase in the same period? Why are our school taxes 29 percent higher than the national average? Why don't we do something about it?

There are six urban areas in New York State that have no school taxes on homes: New York City, Yonkers, Buffalo, Syracuse, Rochester, and Albany. School budgets in these cities are calculated by professionals; these people have recognized that there are more equitable ways to fund schools. Many years ago, before sales or income taxes, property owners were taxed because they were the only ones on record. This is no longer the case. Everyone pays taxes. Everyone benefits from our public schools. Why shouldn't everyone share the cost? We should have a system in place where everyone contributes to school funding.

In those six cities, everyone pays for the schools, and this system is working. There are many different taxes collected, and the schools get a cut of the combined taxes. They also share state and federal aid equally. In Rockland, the state aid is divided eight different ways, with each district receiving a different amount, based on the opinion of the New York State Department of Education's State Aid Office. How do they decide who gets more and who gets less?

Should the value of a house measure the wealth of its owner? In the 1960s through the early 70s, during their income-producing years, a Rockland County couple could buy a house for $40,000. If the value of their property increased because of the proliferation of neighboring McMansions valuing $800,000 and more, why should the assessment go up on the older house? New home assessments should not change the old homeowners' assessments. In California, they have it right: any house, whether new or old, is assessed based on the purchase price at the time it is bought. The assessments of other homes in the area cannot raise a previously built home's assessment by more than 2 percent.

Why doesn't the Rockland County Legislature follow the six big cities in New York State and take over the budgets of all eight school districts in Rockland County? I want to stress that we can make this change without hurting our schools. The Legislature can see to it that all school districts get an equal share. Keep all of the superintendents in their eight school districts, and put a county chancellor in charge of a county board of education. We can have a dedicated income tax, and rid ourselves of these dysfunctional real estate taxes. We can consolidate the eight separate school budgets. Incidentally, these budgets are typically voted on by no more than 10 to 20 percent of eligible voters. Low voter turnout is the reason they pass these crazy budgets.

People reading this article will say that Mr. Miele's been singing his song for a long time. Yes, I have, because I believe in keeping hard-working taxpayers in Rockland. Our real estate taxes are driving out good people. They are spending their pension money in other states, because of the real estate taxes here. We shouldn't forget the senior citizens, the handicapped, the sick, and retirees on a fixed income. They are the foundation of our communities; honoring them supports family values and respect.

Old folks are being edged out by young families that have lots of spending power but not much experience in what makes a good community for their children. A family with two children leaving New York City to settle in Rockland County can get a $750,000 home for free. Read carefully and you will see how. If only they knew that Rockland politicians see them as nothing but fresh taxpayers who can afford higher and higher increases.

Say a husband and wife together are earning $200,000 a year in New York City. They rent a two-bedroom apartment at $4,000 a month, or $48,000 a year, a big expense that is not tax-deductible. If they are sending two children to a private school, at a combined cost of $60,000 a year (also not tax-deductible), their expenses are $108,000 a year. Again, none of this is tax-deductible.

Now, the same family moves to Rockland. If they buy a $750,000 home with a 30-year mortgage at 6 percent interest, the payments come to $4,496.70 per month, or about $54,000 a year. Their payments are mostly tax-deductible. Their school taxes are about $25,000 a year, again, tax-deductible. Together that comes to $79,000 a year. If they are in a 35 percent tax bracket, they get back almost $32,000. In New York City, they were spending $108,000 a year just for rent and school; now they are spending $47,000, or saving $61,000! Isn't that like getting more than a year of New York City rent for free? Of course they don't realize that they are raising taxes for the older homeowners. Every family sets out to do their best; but as people get older and their earning power decreases, they get pushed aside just like those before them.

Why don't the politicians get together and do the right thing for the people? I'd tell any politician to make history and say, "This one is for all of the homeowners." Let's cap property tax increases and keep Rocklanders in Rockland.

———

Senior Citizens Are Suffering because of Unfair Taxes!

November 19, 2009

Why shouldn't senior homeowners qualify for a cap on their property taxes in New York? Elderly couples, living in their Rockland County homes for 40 years and more, are being forced out, because they can't keep up with their real estate taxes. These people worked for many years, kept up their houses, and paid their mortgages and taxes. When they were young, they could afford everything; they planned to finish paying their mortgages, and to live comfortably on their fixed incomes and savings. Now, as they retire, they find that they can't make it on a fixed income in Rockland County. Either they must go back to work or lose their homes. Does New York State want to tell us that's just they way it is?

Today, property taxes alone are more than most senior couples ever paid on their mortgages and income taxes put together. The most recent "stimulus" did nothing for the senior citizens. The politicians took care of themselves, and not the people who put them there. Our representatives took care of helping the corporations out of debt, but left not a dime for the senior citizens. In fact, the government double-crossed the senior citizens. Seniors won't benefit from the Social Security increases of recent years, and now the politicians want to lower Medicare expenditures on old folks.

Retired senior homeowners are struggling to pay their taxes, and no one seems to care. It seems that the Rockland County government, instead of valuing the elderly for their contributions to the community, wants us to move out, if we can't afford it.

The school taxes are particularly unfair to longtime homeowners. The education experts, promoting new programs and constant building and rebuilding, are spending our money, not theirs. Young couples from New York City demand more money for schools or other programs and don't feel the tax increases like we do. They forget that although today's income might support high school taxes, the seniors' income, mostly pension checks based on salaries earned years ago, does not.

We love our homes and want to stay right where we are, next door to you. We would like to help by paying our taxes, but the schools treat us as if we are moneybags. Is it right that we should be forced out of our homes? Is it right that the community we took responsibility for 40 years ago should not take some responsibility for us? Are the politicians and educators truly practicing fiscal responsibility and putting your children first, or are they just throwing our money at programs that will further their own reputations?

Wake up, senior citizens and Rockland County taxpayers! Don't be suckers; don't let people take advantage of you. Get together, maybe create or join a TEA party. Don't just complain, do something about it. Complaining alone means nothing to the politician; to him, it is only a song.

The MTA: Taxation without Representation

July 9, 2009

I've written about the MTA problem several times over the years, and as of today, nothing has changed. It's the same old problem of taxation without representation. The fix is in for the MTA.

Seventeen voting members of the MTA board are nominated by the governor, or recommended by the NYC mayor or the county executives of Nassau, Suffolk, Westchester, Putnam, Dutchess, Rockland, and Orange. Here comes the part I believe is illegal: the representatives from Rockland, Orange, Putnam, and Dutchess counties cast one collective vote; that's right, the "outer counties" get one-quarter vote each! Who in hell came up with this skewed ratio of representation?

There is also a group of "representatives" that I believe do not belong at any of the MTA Board meetings. There are six non-voting, rotating seats held by representatives of organized labor and the "Permanent Citizens Advisory Committee (PCAC)," which serves as a voice for users of MTA transit and commuters' facilities. These representatives do not vote but can speak. The New York State senate confirms this phony board. How come there is no one representing taxpayers on the board? Don't we pay the bills?

The outer counties' payrolls are now going to be taxed to fund the MTA, and there is nothing we can do about it, because our voting power on the board is next to nothing! It's a shame. This gouging was initiated to keep the fares low in New York City. The MTA has been stealing from Rockland and the other outer counties, Orange, Putnam, and Dutchess, for almost 25 years, under the guise of building transportation to and from New York City.

In 1988, the Rockland County Legislature voted unanimously to take over the lease on New Jersey Transit lines passing through Rockland, previously held by the MTA. This was a step in the right direction, because the MTA had lied to us about what it would do for Rockland County. Then someone said, "Let's first have a study." The study cost us $18,000, and the results showed that we should take over the lease, because it would be profitable for Rockland County. But nothing was done! Ten years later, there was a second study, for $18,000 again, to study the MTA situation, with the same results as before. Again, nothing was done, and that failure puts this county in an emergency position today.

Why the second study, with nothing done? Was it just a delaying tactic? Was it for the good of the county, or for politics?

The MTA has a long history of taking advantage of Rockland County taxpayers. Because we fall within the geographic area served by the MTA, we are subject to whatever decision the MTA board makes on how to fund itself, and that includes taxing us however they wish, regardless of how poorly we are served. They have the power to tax us any time they need money. The proof is that now they want to tax our hardworking residents' payroll for their use.

In 2005, the state government in Albany voted to allow the MTA to float the largest bond in history at the time, for $2.9 billion; this was after New Yorkers had voted against a similar bond in 2000. The 2005 bond act was called the "State Renew and Rebuild Transportation Bond Act," but most if not all of the money went to New York City: $450 million to build the Second Avenue Subway, $450 million on LIRR service to Queens, $100 million on a rail linking Kennedy Airport with Queens and

Manhattan. There was no mention of us, here in Rockland. We have been paying our tax dollars since 1986, on our income, on sales, on recorded mortgages, in uncountable use taxes, just to get never-ending studies on a transportation network in Rockland.

The Wall Street bankers who promoted this (and made millions in consulting fees and commissions, no doubt) said the MTA would pay its own way by raising fares. Our state senators and assemblymen's excuse for voting to pass the bond was that the money would come from MTA fares, not taxpayers. It was a lie.

The outer counties were tricked into creating this MTA fiasco, by believing the malarkey that much-needed mass transportation would be brought to the suburbs. It was a fake! All that was brought were studies, studies, and more studies.

The MTA has been collecting taxes from the outer counties since 1986. Altogether, the MTA has collected almost a billion dollars from us. Here's how it breaks down: a 17 percent income tax on any C-corporation, which includes many small businesses; .25 percent tax on all sales in the outer counties; .25 percent tax on all utilities used in our homes and businesses, such as gas, electric, water, and telephone; and .25 percent tax on any new mortgage. Remember when Rockland County removed sales tax, for a time, on clothes under $110? Rocklanders were still obligated to pay the .25 percent sales tax for the MTA. Talk about chutzpah!

The enormous amount of taxes we pay to the MTA is not being properly spent to assist the residents of Rockland County. The MTA concentrates the largest portion of its financial resources and efforts on New York City, Westchester, and even southwestern Connecticut. Here in the outer counties, we haven't seen any new destination train tracks, bus lines, or even trolley cars installed.

Let's get the outer counties out of the MTA. It can be done! The MTA has not done what it said it would with our hard-earned money. It has lied to us and stolen from us. Our politicians have always ended up giving them whatever they want; let's not let it happen this time.

———

The Only Fair Tax

July 18, 2008

At one time, the state sales tax was on luxury items, not on the bare necessities, such as food, shelter, and clothing. Then the sales tax was "upgraded," to include meals purchased at restaurants that provided table service. Later, sales tax was charged even when you served yourself, including take-out food and bottled water. This was called the "hot dog tax"; if the food totaled $1 or less, there was no sales tax added.

Rich or poor, everyone should know what it is to pay taxes. People should know what taxes are for and where they come from. This makes for responsible, fair-minded citizens. Even the needy would not be hurt by a luxury tax if the three necessities of food, shelter, and clothing were tax-free for them.

The unfair tax nowadays is the real estate tax. It's become discriminatory. It is government taking advantage of homeowners.

On the surface, of course, there are good reasons for municipalities to tax real estate. Real estate taxes were initiated for police protection, sanitation, sewers, roads—all property owners' needs, all local services for which homeowners should pay. One of the main reasons for the municipality to exist is to provide local residents with such services. Without the municipality in place, we would rely on the county for all those services. By creating local government and paying property taxes, we gain better services.

Today, though, local government uses property owners to provide higher salaries for themselves, or to enlarge government with new positions by creating programs. Whenever there is a new program, we get hit with higher real estate taxes. This is the easy way out for the municipality. If the government wanted to initiate a new sales tax, luxury tax, or income tax, they would have to go through the New York State Legislature. Many people don't understand this. A New York municipality's only source of revenue that isn't restricted or questioned by higher levels of government is real estate taxes within its jurisdiction. Maybe a village, town, or school district could find other ways of collecting revenue, but raising property taxes is the easiest. Government taxes homeowners because it can.

To expect property owners to pay school, town, village, and county real estate taxes for something other than local services is wrong. When every citizen benefits from a program, every citizen should be included in paying taxes, not just property owners. The homeowner's needs for food, shelter, and clothing should be considered when establishing taxes that are appropriate for homeowners to pay. Many older people are forced out of their homes by exorbitant taxes. I've seen my property taxes go up every year, often by as much as 9 percent.

Schools raise their budgets every year; who pays the increase for the schools? Of course, property owners, even though there are Rockland citizens taking advantage of our school systems and paying no taxes at all. They can vote for school budgets or sit on the school boards. All this, and they do not have to contribute a dime to our schools. Commercial property owners pay enormous school taxes too, and can't even vote in school district elections or on budgets, if they do not live in the school district.

How is it that when all the new buildings, commercial and residential, were going up in Rockland, when sales were breaking all kinds of records, that we had to pay more real estate and sales taxes? With all of this new money coming into the local government and schools, why did government still need to raise sales and real estate taxes every year? And now that property values are going down, will they reduce real estate taxes?

There has to be a way for taxes to be equitable. Why can't we collect a fair tax from all the citizens of Rockland County?

Instead of just taxing homeowners, we should create a county income tax to spread the burden more fairly.

———

New Deal Taxes: Will "Change" Be Any Different?

January 21, 2010

Below are the federal income tax rates that went into effect under Franklin Delano Roosevelt in 1932, and remained in place for over 30 years. Roosevelt's tax rates kept America in a depression until he got us into a war.

Look at these tax rates! They are the reason there was no work. People with money closed down their businesses and retired, shrinking the job market, because it cost too much to stay in business. The unemployment rate was 22 percent until World War II. Most of the jobs that did exist were government or Works Progress Administration positions; otherwise, unemployment would have been more than 60 percent. High taxes created socialism in this country.

President Kennedy dropped the highest tax rate to 72 percent, but made up for it by forcing everyone to pay Social Security. Social Security was created for blue-collar workers. Kennedy then included doctors, lawyers, and white-collar workers. He also brought in all government workers; this gave government workers two pensions. It wasn't until Ronald Reagan became president that the highest income tax rate came down to 28 percent.

Today, looking at how President Obama's "change" has worked so far, I am sure we are on our way back to the Franklin Roosevelt years and another Great Depression.

Schedule II. MARRIED TAXPAYERS FILING JOINT RETURNS and CERTAIN WIDOWS AND WIDOWERS (See page 4).

If the amount on line 11d, page 1, is:		Enter on line 12, page 1:		If the amount on line 11d, page 1, is:		Enter on line 12, page 1:	
Not over $4,000		20% of the amount on line 11d.		$52,000	— $64,000	$21,480, plus 62%	— $52,000
Over—	But not over—		of excess over—	$64,000	— $76,000	$28,920, plus 65%	— $64,000
$4,000	— $8,000	$800, plus 22%	— $4,000	$76,000	— $88,000	$36,720, plus 69%	— $76,000
$8,000	— $12,000	$1,680, plus 26%	— $8,000	$88,000	— $100,000 . . .	$45,000, plus 72%	— $88,000
$12,000	— $16,000	$2,720, plus 30%	— $12,000	$100,000	— $120,000 . . .	$53,640, plus 75%	— $100,000
$16,000	— $20,000	$3,920, plus 34%	— $16,000	$120,000	— $140,000 . . .	$68,640, plus 78%	— $120,000
$20,000	— $24,000	$5,280, plus 38%	— $20,000	$140,000	— $160,000 . . .	$84,240, plus 81%	— $140,000
$24,000	— $28,000	$6,800, plus 43%	— $24,000	$160,000	— $180,000 . . .	$100,440, plus 84%	— $160,000
$28,000	— $32,000	$8,520, plus 47%	— $28,000	$180,000	— $200,000 . . .	$117,240, plus 87%	— $180,000
$32,000	— $36,000	$10,400, plus 50%	— $32,000	$200,000	— $300,000 . . .	$134,640, plus 89%	— $200,000
$36,000	— $40,000	$12,400, plus 53%	— $36,000	$300,000	— $400,000 . . .	$223,640, plus 90%	— $300,000
$40,000	— $44,000	$14,520, plus 56%	— $40,000	$400,000		$313,640, plus 91%	— $400,000
$44,000	— $52,000	$16,760, plus 59%	— $44,000				

ROCKLAND
COUNTY TIMES
ROCKLAND'S OFFICIAL NEWSPAPER SINCE 1888™

| 124th Year, No. 23 | PUBLISHED WEEKLY | 20 PAGES | 75¢ |

Shocking Corruption Charges Levied Against Senate Democrats

Fellow Democrat and Gubernatorial Candidate, Attorney General Andrew Cuomo, Leads Investigation Against Allegedly Crooked Pols

Tempers Flare at Latest North Rockland School Board Meeting

more reserve dollars may yet be used

BY DYLAN SKRILOFF, ERICA ATZL AND LAUREN KATE ROSENBLUM

Government for the People, or Before the People?

The American system of government, in which the judiciary is called upon to check the power of elected officials, and different branches of elected officials are called upon to keep each other honest, used to guarantee that no one was above the law. We are now finding out that our government is not immune to a "payola" system. Is bribery, with cash or favors, the only way to get something done?

Every year we hear about another scandal involving a government official who thought he or she was above the law. In 2006, it was Alan Hevesi, the state comptroller of New York, who used state funds to pay his wife's chauffeur. He had to make a deal to avoid going to jail. A couple of years later it was Elliot Spitzer, who spent thousands on prostitutes while in office, both as attorney general of New York and as governor. In 2010, it's Charlie Rangel, for ethical violations.

Rampant greed also drives the corporations on the stock market to steal from the American people and jeopardize our whole economy, as happened in recent years, when the U.S. government bailed out the biggest stock brokerages and even Fannie Mae. The huge corporate crooks aren't concerned for the financial safety of their country or for their investors, only for their greedy selves. The same goes for the so-called "little guys" like Bernie Madoff, the ones in control of pension funds, and private investments in state, county, and municipal bonds. They make deals with investment firms to benefit themselves, not their clients. Even when they are not committing huge fraud, as Madoff did, they are forever hungry, like maggots, and would double-cross anyone as long as they get want they want: money. The crooked politicians in their pockets should be arrested too.

Instead of catering to their whims, the government should go after these white-collar crooks. Instead of giving them a fine, which they can never fully pay to the losers, give them time in jail. That is the only way they will stop their thievery.

American investors should beware! I also must say, as investors, don't be greedy. The crooks make their money on greedy people.

The musings that follow talk about the ways in which political and corporate greed for power and money are destroying America. Americans must demand fairness, by not letting the pressure to buy and borrow put them in a hole, and by speaking out with their votes.

Greedy Fakers and Crooks

September 16, 2010 (Originally published as "Beware! The Crooks, Creeps, and Phoneys Are Still Around!")

We first published this Musing in 2004, when most Americans still trusted Wall Street and Fannie Mae. The only thing I want to add today is that just as our financial institutions let us down, taking advantage of investors' trust and ignorance, our elected officials can let us down. If they are allowed to do so, it's our country at stake as well as our economy.

Politicians love to make themselves popular by saying that they want to help the needy, the minorities, the poor, and the homeless. They want to help, all right—they want to help themselves. The money intended for the unfortunate is being used to line the pockets of the legal crooks, the fakers, and the greedy ones that have created a bonanza for them.

Let's take Fannie Mae, a mortgage company sanctioned by the U.S. government, which fooled the people it was supposed to help. I remember when Fannie Mae started. Someone who wanted to buy a house valued at $15,000 was given a mortgage for $25,000. The extra $10,000 was put in the hands of real estate brokers for closing costs: commissions, mortgage points, insurance, etc. Low and moderate income families were lured in by the easy money and got stuck, not knowing they would have to pay for other expenses: real estate taxes, insurance, utilities, and repair bills, not to mention high interest rates on their mortgages. The bubble burst around 1971, and many lost their homes when the gasoline crisis created a mini-recession. The real estate business was almost at a standstill, and the mortgage companies and banks were in trouble.

In the 1980s, real estate was moving again. This time, values climbed so fast that houses became worth more than what the owner paid within months. If the owner was in trouble paying his bills, at least he or she could sell to a new buyer.

In 2004, Fannie Mae and Freddie Mac were investigated for "cooking the books," as Armando Falcon, director of the Office of Federal Housing Enterprise Oversight (OFHEO), called it. He charged them with "dipping into the cookie jar," accounting for reserves as assets, and postponing the recognition of expenses to smooth out quarterly earnings. This, Mr. Falcon said, allowed Fannie Mae and Freddie Mac to meet quarterly financial projections and earn large bonuses for their officers and cronies. The bigger the false profit these greedy crooks showed, the bigger the bonuses. Get in there, Armando Falcon! We need more like you! Those people belong in jail.

In 2004, Falcon forced the resignation of Fannie Mae Chairman Franklin Raines, who between 2002 and 2003 took home (I say he stole it) over $35 million, plus $3 million in stock options, according to Mr. Falcon's investigation. This does not include his retirement account, health insurance, or other benefits. Nine other high profile officers at Fannie Mae received bonuses ranging from $3 million to $5 million in 2003. In total, the company awarded $245 million dollars in bonuses over five years.

Help the poor, bunk! Let's tell it like it is: criminals like Raines stole from the poor and gave to the rich, to themselves, and many like them. The real help to the poor came not from executives with big titles, but from public tax dollars siphoned into a "bailout."

———

DROP Beneficiaries: Legal Crooks?

March 4, 2010

Government employees: want to retire rich, at the taxpayers' expense, and drive your city, county, and state government broke? Just join a DROP, it's legal.

DROP, or the Deferred Retirement Option Plan, rewards government employees and screws the taxpayers. The idea is to entice older, more experienced government workers, eligible for early retirement, to stay on the job by offering bigger pensions if they stay. The hope is to make lower-paying government jobs more competitive with the salaries of the private sector. This allows so-called hard-to-replace teachers, policemen, firemen, engineers and other public workers to stay on the job instead of retiring.

DROP is supposed to work this way: a government employee eligible for early retirement agrees to work for five more years without getting a raise. In the meantime, the pension that he would have gotten paid, if he had retired, is put into a DROP account which bears high interest. In five years, when he retires, he can opt to take the value of his DROP account as a lump sum, or leave the principal untouched, and take the monthly interest payments. Upon retirement he will also receive his weekly or monthly pension check, calculated at the rate he would have begun receiving five years ago.

But who thought this next part up? Some of the DROP accounts have been set up to guarantee as much as 9 percent interest, more than double the earnings of 2010 private-sector investment accounts, or double the 2010 market rate! DROP retirees in cities like San Diego, Philadelphia, Milwaukee, and Houston are taking monthly DROP payouts that are up to 1.5 times their salaries, while it remains impossible for their employer, the government, to earn that kind of money on its DROP investments. The taxpayers have to pick up the balance.

Here are some examples of what DROP is costing taxpayers in some large U.S. cities.

In 2003, the Texas Legislature approved a constitutional amendment barring cities in Texas from reducing pensions. In Houston, the city pension fund suddenly could not support the payouts, and ended up owing $1.5 billion in benefits to the work force.

In San Diego, the shortfall was over $2 billion as of February, 2009. Retirees were guaranteed 7.5 percent interest on their DROP accounts. According to the San Diego Union-Tribune, San Diego City Council records showed that at least 5 city retirees had DROP accounts "topping $1 million, while scores of others topped $500,000." In addition, San Diego workers were entitled to set up a retirement plan in which their contributions were matched by taxpayers!

In Philadelphia recently, the elected officials thought up an even sweeter plan for themselves. Not only could they enroll in DROP, but if re-elected, they could retire for a day, then resume collecting a salary, while still taking DROP retirement payments. The mayor said the benefits were draining the pension fund, and should be abolished. No way, said the city pension trustees; then they made the benefits permanent.

In Milwaukee, local news described how elected politicians were qualifying for retirement payouts of $1 million or more. Also, like the Philadelphia "retire-for-a-day" schemers, some Milwaukee government employees were allowed to continue working past their planned retirement date, and continued taking DROP payments in addition to their salaries. County Executive F. Thomas Ament put his own $35,000 monthly pension in place as well, leading to his forced resignation. Seven members of the County Board of Supervisors were ousted in a recall vote, following the Milwaukee scandal.

When these DROP scandals broke, the politicians used a perfect excuse: "It's not our fault, it's the recession." In other words, although they were the ones who guaranteed the return rates for DROP without regard for the possibility that the market would change, once it did change, they should not be blamed for poor planning. They never blame themselves. After all, it's not their money. They can put us taxpayers in a worse condition to pay these pensions, and it costs them nothing.

———

Use Your Vote! Keep the Politicians Honest!

March 11, 2010 (originally published under the title, "Use Your Vote! People Power Works!")

In 1986, Ronald Reagan said, "I've always felt the nine most terrifying words in the English language are, 'I'm from the government, and I'm here to help.'" He understood the growing mistrust that Americans had, at the time, for their government.

The Reagan days are gone. Ronald Reagan brought America back from the time when the socialist Jimmy Carter almost ruined our country. We lost the respect of the European countries during Carter's presidency, and this loss of legitimacy is happening again today, thanks to President Obama and his partners. He and his cohorts are definitely socialists, and if we do nothing we will become a communist country. Obama mentioned he wanted a "civilian national security force", which sounds dangerous. A communist takeover needs power, and his idea of a national security force could be his way to get there. Few struggling taxpayers do anything to help themselves.

People forget that the most important votes cast in government are their own. They either don't vote, or always vote the same way, causing incumbent politicians to get comfortable and lazy. The politicians take ever-higher salaries, get pension plans, and take long vacations, on the taxpayers' dollar, and all they have to do is fool the people into voting for them over and over. Years ago, politicians didn't even get paid, or took only a token salary. It was a privilege to serve. But most politicians today never had a paying job out of office, or hold office for their whole lives, which is not right.

Since 1982, 2,958 elections have been held in New York State for individual senate and assembly seats, and only 39 times incumbents lost. In 2008, 212 combined incumbent senators and assemblymen won 80 percent of the vote— that's right, 80 percent—and 57 ran unopposed. No wonder they feel they can break promises to voters or take advantage of their office. They are almost guaranteed to be re-elected. There should be a limit to how many times a politician can run. Let's get together and break them up, so they can find jobs and go to work as we do. Now is the time, before it is too late. The people, when united, are more powerful than any government.

Get involved! The power of the people works. Save your future, and your children's. Although taxpayers pay the bills, we are not organized. We vote for either a party or the brand name with the best commercials, like Obama. He promised everything, a big change. Has he kept his promise? People, remember: the right and privilege most important to your freedom is the right to vote. Don't vote for the party or a rock star, but for the person you can trust.

The flamboyant Jimmy Walker, mayor of New York City in the 1920s, famously remarked, "Will the voters remember in November what I did in May?" Taxpaying citizens, again and again I stress: the people alone can save America. Bring America back!

———

Lawyers: Are They Just Out for Money?

March 18, 2010

I always had the highest respect for lawyers, and considered them to be pillars of our society. Being sworn to uphold the Constitution and the rule of law within our court system is an honor, and an expression of trust in our country.

Sometimes, though, we find lawyers using the system to flaunt the laws, to gain power and money. To me these are criminals, abusing their positions of legal authority. These abusers hate any kind of government regulation; after all, they know the laws, and no one can tell them what is right and what is wrong. One government proposal requires lawyers who know of fraud committed by their corporate clients to expose the fraud, to the client's managers or board. Some of the lawyers affected claim that if they have to report fraud, they might have to withdraw from a client. It would hinder their business.

These are greedy lawyers, hiding behind their trusted degrees. They are in law solely for the money, and the heck with society—they'll get theirs, and let the rest of society fend for themselves. These lawyers know the system, and use it for their own selfish reasons.

There are also lawyers who hide behind the very noble idea that everyone should be defended to the fullest, no matter what. But how far do you take it?

When a lawyer interviews a client, I'm sure he has an idea of whether the case is likely to succeed on sound legal grounds. Once the lawyer comes to this conclusion, is it the money or the law that governs how he handles the case? An honest lawyer, wanting to uphold his professional oath, will refuse to be part of a case in which the client asks him to do something dishonest or obstructive of justice. He will also refuse to take a client whose claim is shaky, or not worth the client's expense. A lawyer in it for the money alone, with no concern for the rule of law or society, will take any client who can pay the retainer fee. Now, the client has to continue to pay as the case goes on. It can take many years of getting nowhere before the client gets tired or runs out of money, finally has to pay the lawyer to settle the case, and finds out that he's worse off than he was in the beginning. The only winner of the case was the lawyer. He gets paid, win or lose.

I know of a case where there was a fight in a building, between two men, about a woman. The landlord had nothing to do with this fight, and rarely went to the building. The big bully in the fight got hurt, and found a lawyer to sue the landlord and his corporation for $15 million. The reason to sue for that crazy amount was to put fear into the defense, and to give the client a false sense of the case's importance, so the lawyer could justify a larger retainer fee.

These types of lawyers are filling the courts with frivolous cases, with no basis whatsoever in the law. A while ago, Governor Pataki signed a bill to eliminate the mention of damage amounts in liability suits during the filing process. The lawyer is now allowed to specify a damage figure only during opening or closing arguments.

The insurance companies and courts should carefully review cases; lawyers who bring frivolous cases should be immediately punishable with sanctions by law. Such cases shouldn't have to go through the whole court system. It can be expensive, and that's what crooked lawyers count on. A crooked lawyer is not interested in winning the case, but in being a big enough nuisance to the defendant and the insurance company that he can expect a monetary settlement. In England, the loser in a "deep pockets" lawsuit has to pay all the expenses of the court and the defendant, as well as his lawyer.

At one time, lawyers couldn't advertise as they do today. Today every ambulance chaser can put an ad on the cover of the phone book. I call it bunk. "Free consultation! No Recovery, No Fee!" Who are they kidding? Read the fine print on the contract before you hire one of these guys—whether it's in photocopy expenses or paralegal services, they'll find a way to take your money, even if you win.

———

Gas Gouging

March 18, 2010

In 1948, a friend and I took an exciting auto trip from New York City to Miami, Florida, a 1,350-mile drive. We kept records of our expenses on the trip. The spending for gas and oil for the entire trip was $12.50. Gas cost approximately 16 cents a gallon; you did about 28 miles to a gallon; and there were no tolls.

In the year 1967, I paid 23 cents a gallon. The price had risen about 7 cents a gallon in about 20 years. In 2010, gasoline costs around $3 per gallon, and the price is still climbing. If a car gets (you hope) 25 miles per gallon, and accounting for the tolls you'd now have to pay, the same trip to Florida would cost closer to $300 in 2010, nearly 20 times what it cost in 1947.

I know what you readers are thinking. With the increase of inflation, this is not news. In 1948, the Dow Jones climbed to a record-breaking 190 points; in 2010, it was over 10,000. But I still think we're being ripped off.

When gasoline prices started to climb, gas stations started to take service away from their customers. The gas station attendant used to check your oil and the air in your tires, and clean your windshield. Don't forget the free map that was available for the asking. In the 1940s, when you filled your gas tank, you paid two singles and always received change. Twenty years later, it was a five-dollar bill, and you received change. Not much longer after that, it became a 10-dollar bill, and again, you received change. In the equivalent 2010 car you need a 50-dollar bill to fill your tank, with no service and no courtesy. There's no more checking the air in your tires, checking your oil, or cleaning your windshield. In New York, they don't even pump the gasoline into your car.

The wonderful idea behind the disappearance of full-service gas stations in most states was keeping the price of gas down for the public. That is bunk. What it did, during the gas crisis in the 70s, was take away thousands of jobs and take away the service. Today in New Jersey, by law, every gas station must have an attendant to fill your tank. There are thousands getting paid to fill all of the auto tanks, yet the gasoline is almost 40 cents a gallon less than here in New York. In fact, it's been reported that New Jersey has the lowest gasoline prices in the United States. What is happening here?

I believe that gas gouging has become normal, in the sense that it's become business as usual for the gas industry to continually find new ways to take advantage of the public. Originally, gasoline stations did not depend on gasoline alone for making a good profit. Their main income was on services and products sold at the station. Today, the gasoline stations can rely solely on gasoline sales, because profits are very high. Gasoline is considered a necessity; any gas station, with good or bad service, is guaranteed a certain amount of profit.

My reason for this little story is to blame all of this gouging on the U.S. government. The government could stop this by simply putting the brakes on the price a gasoline station can charge. I believe that government should avoid enacting price controls in a capitalist society, but gasoline in this country belongs to the people. I remember saying at the time of the 1970s gasoline crisis, "The gas stations do not own the gasoline. We do." The American taxpayers and the Armed Forces, together, provide the money and manpower to safeguard the United States' access to energy and fuel.

Oil in this country belongs to all Americans, and that means the price of gasoline should not be different at different pumps. I believe the price of oil is one cost that should be controlled by the government, and the pump prices should show it. That is one way to ensure that the gas industry stops taking advantage of Americans.

––––––

Fake Recessions and Back-door Socialism

February 5, 2009 (originally published under the title, "Fake Recessions and the Redistribution of Wealth")

In the 20 years from 1988 to 2008, Rockland County's population grew 15 percent, and the number of restaurants increased tenfold. On Route 59 between Tallman and Nanuet, we have three McDonald's restaurants, two Wendy's, a Roy Rogers, a White Castle, and I am sure I left some out. Nail parlors didn't even exist in Rockland in 1988. Neither did the Palisades mega-mall, with its theaters, restaurants, and hundreds of chain stores. Need a supermarket? Rockland has them coming and going. Hardware? We have two Home Depots, one Lowes in operation, and another being built next to Costco in Nanuet, more than double the size of the first. Two Barnes and Noble stores—do people read all of these books? Let's not forget the office supply stores; how many Staples, Office Maxes, and Office Depots are there in Rockland, anyway?

Are we really in a recession, and if so, who is it affecting? I ride in my car and the traffic is crazy, I go to a mall and it is packed. Many businesses are doing great. So I wonder, is it a recession, or is it another excuse for a redistribution of wealth, which is just a backdoor route to socialism?

Large corporations have been overextended for so long that I'm sure a lot of them have stopped keeping up with their bills. To stay viable, big public corporations must sell more shares every year and keep their paper value up. In order to do this, they must show how well they are growing, even when the new business isn't there. They force growth, by borrowing from large banks and lending institutions. They use the money on new construction, or to create new jobs to show that they are thriving, then struggle to pay interest on billions of borrowed dollars. I believe that the government used the recession angle for a long time as an excuse to bail out large corporations. By dropping interest rates, the government kept the stock market from going belly-up. Didn't our leaders learn anything from the Alan Greenspan disaster?

The so-called brains, Alan Greenspan, had the idea to save the economy by dropping interest rates. He dropped them 11 times in one year, down to 1.75 percent, which was less than the existing inflation rate. Then Ben Bernanke took his place, and continued to drop interest rates and screw up the mortgage market, all for the benefit of the stock market, the huge corporations, and the crooked investment banks. Don't let them fool you; they did this for the stock market. Did you see how much the stock market grew? Low interest rates provided easy money for large corporations, or for anyone who could afford to play the stock market. This was also a bonanza for the mortgage market, for crooked real estate brokers, and housing developers, who overvalued homes to get their money. Stockbrokers enticed clients with high-interest-rate subprime mortgages on the overvalued houses. People went wild to get in on the action with the overbuilding and easy money.

If there was a recession as a result, it didn't bother the corporations and the stockbrokers; it hurt small businesses and the regular working people. Greenspan hurt the seniors on fixed incomes, he hurt their retirement plans, and he hurt the workers who relied on their investments for retirement. He dropped the interest rates so low that people with savings accounts were actually losing money. Figure it out, if inflation is about 3 percent and you get, say, 1 percent interest on your savings, then by paying taxes on the interest you are losing money! These people didn't deserve to get hurt. The government used their taxable dollars to bail out the big corporations. Isn't that a redistribution of wealth?

Of course it also felt like a recession for the working person who overextended himself. Here's a great example I read about. A family bought their home for $100,000. The home's value rose to $900,000 and the owners decided to borrow $600,000 dollars against it. With the money they borrowed, the jerks went wild, bought a Lexus, went on vacations, anything just to spend the cash, because they thought they had a bonanza. They are now in foreclosure, and can't sell their house for the mortgage of $600,000. These are the type of people that got in trouble, and they want us to bail them out and feel sorry for them. I repeat, isn't this redistribution of wealth? The government got involved in saving them, once again, with our taxes. They called it the "Economic Stimulus Act of 2008," and it was estimated to cost the government over $152 billion.

So inflation, recession, de-flation, call it whatever you want, the United States economy is now based on doling taxpayer dollars out to those who squander big money on bad risks. When taxpayers are doing well, the government distributes their wealth to the "less fortunate," and everything starts all over again. The government never learns. They want to do the same thing in 2009. Stop and think, are we stepping into socialism through the back door? In 2008, it was hundreds of billions of dollars to bail out the banks, today a new "stimulus" is projected to cost over $1 trillion. When in hell are people going to learn?

ROCKLAND
COUNTY TIMES
ROCKLAND'S OFFICIAL NEWSPAPER SINCE 1888™

124th Year, No. 23   PUBLISHED WEEKLY   20 PAGES   75¢

Orangetown Defeats Affordable Housing on 4-1 Vote

Over 300 residents jam Town Hall for public hearing

BY ROBERT KNIGHT
CITY EDITOR
ROCKLAND COUNTY TIMES

"Overflow Crowd" ▮ More than 300 Orangetown residents showed up at Monday Night's Town Hall public hearing on affordable housing.

Tea Party Movement Maintains Momentum with Tax Day Protests

RFA Tax Day Tea Party Protesters in Rockland County Oppose Big Gov't

BY LILY BETJEMAN

"Tea Scene" ▮ Ombase rikes outside the Rockland County Courthouse April 15

"Patriot" ▮ A first time Tea Party attendee stakes his ground on the lawn

Above, Left and Below Right:
Rockland County Times
reports on voter activism,
candidate response.

• • • • •

Below Left: My campaign vehicle,
1995, was well-equiped to let
voters hear the facts.

Second Round of Debates

"Debate" ▮ Stony Point Town Council and Supervisor candidates pictured at their initial debate on September 29. Candidates gathered again on October 6 to discuss issues affecting the lives of town residents and will do so once more on October 27.

Your Vote

An American Liberty, Not a Ticket to a Party

If we truly want to uphold the American founders' principle of government by the people, we have to take our voting more seriously than we do. It's not all about party loyalty, or about following the person with the most charisma. President Obama, for instance, was elected by the young, and by good Democrats who blindly voted for the man waving the Democratic Party's flag. Norman Podhoretz, a Jewish conservative writer, describes how Jewish Americans vote for the Democratic Party as a block in his book, "Why Are Jews Liberals?" They voted 78 percent for Obama, and I'm sure they are sorry they did.

It was a similar story with other communities of loyal Democrats in this country: the academics, the union laborers, even the career Democrats. You are all suffering because of Obama's lies. To save your families and our country, you must vote for a person, and not just a Democrat. In Germany, Hitler came into power with only 35 percent of the votes by blaming the Jews for all of Germany's problems.

Obama, instead of blaming a race of people, blames the older folks, saying they're old-fashioned, and that we need a "change". Notice, most of the college kids are saying the same thing. What else can I say? Obama is using the young to take over the United States without firing a bullet.

The ACORN issue alone should tell you who your president is. ACORN, the Association of Community Organizations for Reform Now, has been tied to Barack Obama since 1992. In that year, he headed a voter registration effort for ACORN called Project Vote. He did so well that they made him a trainer for ACORN'S Chicago conferences. In 1995, he represented ACORN in court. In 2007, as he embarked on his presidential bid, he gave ACORN a list of his campaign donors, and the following year, he gave $832,000 to ACORN's Project Vote. In the same year, the year of Obama's election to the U.S. Presidency, 400,000 out of 1.3 million voter registrations ACORN turned in were found to be duplicates or fraudulent. That's right—Obama's pet project used huge donations given by him and his supporters, and it nearly ended in an electoral disaster.

Until real change comes to our local communities, seniors should demand their due from Obama and his administration. He removed 2010's Social Security raise for old folks, and now he wants to remove $500 billion from Medicare. He says it affects "only" all of us who have been paying taxes for more than 50 years.

What about the blue-collar workers, small businesses, and family businesses, who pay the bulk of this country's taxes? Why haven't Obama and his cronies in local government capped or reduced their taxes?

Today we have a reverse economy: instead of being able to build futures for themselves, the taxpayers are public servants. They are not guaranteed any income, only more taxes, as they struggle to keep or gain better jobs, and to keep or grow their businesses. They are saddled with increasing taxes of all kinds, on their income, on their homes, and on their businesses. All this digs into whatever profits they make. Also, why in heavens does every business, no matter how small, get charged extra taxes for utilities like water, sewer, and telephone? When will Obama and his local supporters address the wasteful spending that is responsible for the tax increases?

Some examples of wasteful spending are the government employees' yearly raises and increased benefits, at the taxpayers' expense, no matter what the inflation rate or whether there is a recession. This is nothing less than a government union, which at one time was against the law. Our politicians give them whatever they want, and it never ends. Today's economy cannot support this kind of spending. If we don't cap spending, private sector jobs will disappear, and welfare will again be on the rise.

Some of these musings were written during Obama's presidential campaign, and some during his administration. My goal was to get readers to vote responsibly, not for imaginary change, not for a rock star, but for a leader who puts hard-working, taxpaying Americans first.

It didn't happen in 2008. My hope for the nation is that the next time around, people will listen.

Who Are the Voters?

November 5, 2009

Who are the voters? Some are young college students who copy their professors. They follow the campaign action like kids playing follow the leader. There are also voters that latch onto any dumb entertainer, always looking for the most-publicized cause in the media. When their candidate wins, they feel they have made it to stardom.

Then there are older people, who know the issues and have been there in the action, building the country and their families. We vote for the person we believe will protect your future.

America has eradicated communism and dictatorships from Iraq, Pakistan, Germany, France, Japan, Israel, Italy, Korea, the Philippines; the list goes on and on. At the same time, Americans are tolerating the new "changes" in our own country, not seeing that what we eradicated in foreign countries is being created here. Change for what? Change against the American culture, belief in family values, religion, and our great country? The worst change is the belittling attitude among Americans toward our troops, who are fighting to save the freedom of suffering people.

During the Great Depression, the Communist Party in New York City had control of leadership roles. To get a job or enter a program, you were told to join the Communist Party. One acquaintance of mine did just that. Years later his son was denied a position with the New York City Police Department because of that old communist association.

Yet the New York City Communists really didn't know what a communist country was. They used the name because at the time, communists in Russia helped the people to overthrow the Czar. The working people in this country didn't realize that after overthrowing the Czar, the Russian Communists took over all the people's wealth themselves. Is this what the "change" in America is all about? People want to "share the wealth"? Go to any communist country, and you will see that the wealth is not shared.

Once World War II started, the Communist Party was outlawed in New York. Its members had to go somewhere, so they created the Liberal Party. The Liberal Party in New York is now on its way out; they are no longer on the ballot. Instead, they took over the Democratic Party in New York City. It was easy; they disguised their candidate as a Democrat, and got him or her into a primary.

The best example was when the liberal wing of the Democratic Party ran a primary against Mayor Koch in 1989. Koch didn't agree with the liberals. He said they were never satisfied, and this was his downfall. The liberals put up Dinkins, who became the worst Mayor ever, who didn't even pay his income taxes. I attended one of Mayor Koch's fundraisers, and he said, "Just vote in the primary, and the rest is easy to win." The liberals have power in the Democratic Party only because they all vote in the primary, and the regular party members don't.

Today, the same thing is going on within the National Democratic Party. Real Democrats should recognize that unruly demonstrators are a disguised party, and are infiltrating the National Democratic Party. The Democratic Party is becoming vulnerable to destruction, and if Democrats don't wake up the party will be history.

The Democratic Party I always knew were believers in America first. Think of what has happened to U.S. Senator Joe Lieberman, of Connecticut. Here was a true Democrat, who voted more than 95 percent with the Democratic Party. He voted against his party once, for the Iraq War, and the ultra-liberal wing of the Democratic Party ran a primary against him in 2006. Even Senator Clinton did not support him. As a result, he lost the nomination that year.

If you want to cook a lobster, don't put it in hot water. It will jump out. Instead, put it in cold water then slowly turn up the fire. The lobster will be comfortable at first, and then become cooked. The Democrats in this country, like political lobsters, are getting slowly cooked in lies. Elected Democrats are becoming obstructionists, voting against their own policies when it suits whatever image they are trying to create for the next election. Are they destroying the Democratic Party without knowing it? The terrorists and America-haters will be rejoicing if the Democratic Party falls prey to the sotto voce that agitates for the liberal agenda.

Obama Is Not a Democrat, Is Using Voters

October 9, 2008

Obama is not a true American. He wants to be the head of the anti-Americans by using his "change" slogan. Democrats, you are being used! The American fool who helps him by voting for him is destroying his or her own American family by bringing socialism, which will be followed by communism.

Look at his connections: Frank Marshall Davis, his communist mentor in Hawaii, and Reverend Jeremiah Wright, who supports radical Islamist Louis Farrakhan, and preaches anti-white, anti-American sermons. Obama attended Farrakhan's anti-American Million Man March on Washington in 1995. Another associate, William Ayers, was the leader of the Weather Underground. This group of extremists bragged about bombing police stations in New York and San Francisco in 1970, the Pentagon in 1972, and in 1975, the Truman building, which houses the U.S. State Department. Obama had close ties with Ayers for over 20 years in Chicago. Should we forgive him for these connections? If so, should we forgive the 9/11 terrorists?

The list goes on. Obama supported Raila Odinga, the radical socialist prime minister of Kenya, who came to power amid Islamist violence and church burnings, in his run for the presidency of Kenya. Obama even campaigned for him in Kenya. Obama has been influenced by men like Frantz Fanon, Stokely Carmichael, and Malcolm X, all anti-white, and by many accounts anti-semitic, revolutionaries. Jesse Jackson and

Al Sharpton, who always blame white people, both support Obama.

Obama wants to change America, but he can't change those connections to communists, radical anti-American terrorists, and hate mongers.

His policies show more of who he is. In Illinois, he voted to teach sex education to all school children from kindergarten through age 12. He supports the so-called "Freedom of Choice" act, a Federal law that was recently changed to allow a pregnant minor to get an abortion without telling a parent. The old law expressly required parental notification. Why support a bill that removes that requirement?

Look at his crazy socialist tax idea too. At an income less than $250,000, you would not have to pay income tax at all. Everyone making over $250,000 would pay federal income tax for the whole country. Here is a person who went to the top schools, including Columbia University and Harvard Law School, but never had a job outside of politics and political organizing. His ideas didn't come from working and living in the America we know. He knows what he's learned from leftist politicians, and socialist and communist academics. Either he has no clue what his ideas will do to America, or he doesn't care.

———

Sarah Palin, a True American Leader

September 11, 2008

When Sarah Palin, then-governor of Alaska, was named as John McCain's running mate for his presidential campaign, the critics declared her unqualified before she even had a chance to speak for herself. Some of the loudest were those who insisted that as a mother of five, she would be either unable to perform the duties of a vice president, or would put the welfare of her family before the welfare of the country.

Is it possible that in the years since professional women began working in this country, people don't understand what drives someone like Sarah Palin? This is a woman with leadership in her blood, with a fighting heart, who cannot be still when she sees working people being taken advantage of and held down.

Here is a woman who graduated from college in journalism and was a former beauty queen. At the age of 28, was she qualified for a seat on the Wasilla City Council? Was she qualified to reform a corrupt local government that was taking advantage of those they were supposed to serve? She didn't have to get into politics. She already had a job, and in fact was already admired as a public figure in journalism. But Sarah Palin stood up to do something for the people when no one else would.

From a seat on the Wasilla, Alaska City Council, where she opposed tax increases and wasteful government spending, was she qualified to run for mayor? Yet after she was elected, she dropped three property taxes during her time in office, and destroyed the former mayor's machine of government cronies that had been in place for many years.

I know a little about politics from my experiences running for office in Rockland County, and believe me, this kind of upset is unheard of. The opposition Mrs. Palin faced must have been not only tremendous, but frightening. Remember, this was a woman who had no sure thing to gain from this fight but a bunch of headaches, or worse. Some of these politicians can really ruin you once they set themselves against you. Mrs. Palin did not let this stop her. She saw an injustice, and she knew she had to do something about it.

Mrs. Palin could have stopped there. After all, she was married and comfortable, a "supermom" who was prominent in the community, and she had achieved her purpose of clearing corruption out of her hometown. Surely she wasn't qualified to do more than that? She could have listened to the voices of critics who hinted that as a Christian woman, she should set an example by focusing on her family.

But something in Sarah Palin would not allow her to hold back when there was a fight to take on. She accepted an appointment to Alaska's Oil and Gas Commission in 2003, and promptly set out to expose corrupt relationships between the state and the big oil companies. She resigned in protest in 2004, and participated in an investigation against a member of her own Republican Party, which resulted in his being fined $12,000. She went so far as to cross party lines to participate in an ethics complaint by the state Democrats against Alaska Attorney General Gregg Renkes, which forced his resignation.

Shouldn't Mrs. Palin's qualifications have stopped there? After only ten years in politics, she had forced the state government into accountability for irresponsible spending. She was 40 years old, the mother of four children, and again, could have opted for a quieter life—some would even say, a more respectable one. Instead, she saw the opportunity to oppose the Republican machine running Alaska's government, which was in bed with the big oil companies at the people's expense. She forced a primary against the governor in 2005.

I've been in the position that Mrs. Palin was in, with the party against me, but the people wanting me to run. It's no easy task to force a primary, let alone win. Here in Ramapo, the party opposition got so ugly that three Republican mayors actually endorsed the Democratic incumbent to run against me in the primary. But when the people spoke, and asked me to stand up for them, they didn't ask whether I was qualified. They only knew that I would fight for them. I'm sure it was even worse for Sarah Palin. Here in Rockland, we have gangs of old-guard politicians, but she had that and more against her. Her opposition had not only state money behind them, but also the power of big oil.

Like Ramapo residents, the people of Alaska did not comb Mrs. Palin's resume for qualifications. When they spoke through their votes, she won a three-way primary, beating the incumbent with 51 percent of the votes, while he only got 19 percent. She was elected governor of Alaska in 2006, and immediately began working to clear corruption out of the state government as she had in her own hometown, and as she had in the state oil commission.

One of the first things Mrs. Palin did as governor was to sell the governor's private jet. She did all her commuting by state-owned car or by commercial airline, to show her commitment to end wasteful spending. Next on the bill was to tackle state policies on energy, specifically the prospect of building a new pipeline from Alaska to the lower 48 states. This was a project that had been stalled for years because of a deadlock in the state legislature. Mrs. Palin got the legislation passed, and two pipelines are underway, expected to be completed by 2013.

Sarah Palin got more done, in less than 15 years in politics, than most political leaders accomplish in a lifetime. And now her critics want to tell her, as I'm sure they have told her over and over, from the time she got her first job, that she should go home, that she is not qualified! This is nothing more than jealousy. Her critics should be ashamed of trying to keep this fighting woman down.

I have one more point to make, and I hope that parents will share this with their children of voting age. Be careful about voting for a man whose "qualifications" prove nothing more than that he will be a puppet for the Democratic party, which is run right now by a handful of liberal socialist leaders. Years ago, Winston Churchill said that under the age of 30, any person who is not a socialist has no heart; but anyone who is a socialist over the age of 30 has no head. Right now, you may have no expenses in the sense of food, shelter, and clothing, which is all paid by your parents. You pay no taxes. Think about what life will be like when you are on your own, and then think again about whether you want to vote for a rock star.

Vote for the Person, Not the Party!

October 30, 2009

Your local election this year should not be overshadowed by the doings of the president. Our last federal election had to do with political parties only, and mostly with which party was more entertaining. As a result, we have a president who is almost never in his office, and uses our tax money to continue campaigning all over the country, like an actor. He's a good actor. He fooled the Democrats, the Independents, and some Republicans too; now he's fooling his staff and all those who believed in his campaign for "change". He changed the country, all right. To me the White House looks like a gang of mice taking orders from a Cinderella president. Last year's voters either never voted before or liked free entertainment.

The "change" campaign was interesting: the new candidates claimed to have better ideas, and the incumbents should have gone on alert, but they didn't. Well, many newcomers won; but have they lived up to the challenge they set for themselves? Have they proven themselves to be leaders, and not just entertainers?

Last year's voters should be congratulated for getting to the polls, but they didn't vote seriously. They got swept up in something more like a Broadway or Hollywood production. They forgot that voting is the American mark of liberty.

When we vote, we show the non-Americans and terrorists that they can never take our freedom away from us, no matter what. I've said it many times: to vote is a right, and we free people have to honor our armed forces by not letting anyone take it away.

The people who didn't vote have nothing to quack about. They'd be ashamed if they'd only stop and think for a moment. How would you feel, and what would you do, if someone took your vote away from you?

This year, take your voting seriously. Vote for the person you think is most qualified; this is not a beauty contest, nor about canonizing a saint. If you don't know whether your candidate is qualified, you are voting for a party or for an actor.

I say it again: when you vote for a party, you are being used. Try it. Vote for a person. If you don't know the person's qualifications, leave that position on the ballot blank. If you feel discouraged, looking at your blank ballot, resolve now to get to know the people who will appear on next year's ballot. Voting for a party will fill up your ballot and give you a false sense of security, just as buying a popular brand of cereal fools you into believing you are buying good nutrition. But in the end, voting for a party gets you nowhere.

Voters, remember, to the victors go the spoils. Ask yourselves whether your candidate can really deliver all the promises he or she made while running for office. Think about what issues are important to you; don't worry about what's popular. Will taxes rise again? How will this candidate deal with the environment, spend your money, or lead in times of catastrophe, when the system stalls? When times get tight, will this candidate have the courage to cut services, and not to raise taxes to cover mistakes? It is difficult to say, because only time will tell; but you can and must pick the best possible candidate.

To the victors, just remember: don't embarrass the voters. You must be honest to yourselves, God, your country, and all American citizens.

I want to repeat: Vote, Vote, Vote! And do not vote just for the party. Vote for the person. If you don't know the person running for office, leave a blank. Pay attention, so that next year, you will know the candidates better, and be able to cast your vote wisely.

God bless America.

———

School Budget Elections Are Coming Up — VOTE!

May 8, 2010

Your local school budget election is coming up. This is more important than voting for President of the United States.

Remember, your public officials will not help you if you are not willing to get out and vote. Voting is the only statement they understand. When there are more than 20,000 eligible voters in a school district and only 2,000 come out to vote, those who didn't vote shouldn't complain. You have done it to yourselves. Instead of complaining, take action. When you don't go to the polls, you vote against yourself; it counts as two votes for your adversary. Remember folks, every vote counts.

The TEA Party has it right: taxpayers have to get together and vote, to make themselves heard. Every year, there is an increase in school taxes that exceeds the inflation rate. We homeowners are not united as voters when it comes to the schools, and as a result we are discriminated against and taken advantage of. Home value does not measure one's wealth, income, or expenses, or most of all, the ability of a homeowner to bring in the money they need to pay increasing taxes. Why didn't the real estate taxes go down when our home values went down?

Having the school budgets in place is very important; every American benefits when children get excellent public school educations.

But shouldn't everyone share in the expense? If we did, maybe everyone would be more conscientious about how the money was being spent. No one's minding the store, and as a result, there is a lot of waste in the budget. Those who make the budgets every year should start at zero. Instead, they leave in what was budgeted in years past for major repairs, equipment, supplies, etc. This should be investigated. Don't use the teachers' salaries as an excuse when the budget goes up; they are united and they make their issues heard. Get involved and know where and how your tax dollars are being spent. Is an increase really for the classrooms? For administration? Or is it for an obsolete or dreamed-up expense?

EXTRA! EXTRA! On April 29, 2010, the Wall Street Journal reported, "Hundreds of school districts across New York have violated state law by stockpiling billions of dollars that could have been used to lower property taxes... [D]istricts have tucked away that money in an array of obscure reserve funds totaling $3.3 billion, according to a recent state estimate." State law allows for school districts to keep a rainy-day fund in case of need, but that amount must not top 4 percent of a district's annual budget. That's right-the state comptroller has discovered for a fact that school districts across the state have been keeping back billions in surplus funds, in excess of 4 percent of the annual budgets!

Now do you want to find out what's going on in your school district? Mark your calendar. Call your friends and neighbors, and get out and vote. No matter how you vote, just show that you have an interest in your school budget.

This month, the increase in school taxes will hit you. You may only see it as a small increase in your monthly mortgage payments; it may not seem like much. Just remember that it goes up a little every year. Every increase leads to the next one.

ROCKLAND
COUNTY TIMES
ROCKLAND'S OFFICIAL NEWSPAPER SINCE 1888™

124th Year, No. 23   PUBLISHED WEEKLY   20 PAGES   75¢

Rockland and Orange County Leaders Lash Out at MTA Board

Egregious Service Cuts bring Unanimous Condemnation from Officials

BY DYLAN SKRILOFF
MANAGING EDITOR
ROCKLAND COUNTY TIMES

Flanked by a security contingent that a U.S. Senator would envy, a handful of members of the MTA Board sat and withstood a

Piperato Swears in 79 New Citizens

Rockland County Clerk Paul Piperato hosted a naturalization ceremony on Friday, June 3, 2011 at 10:30 a.m., at the Provincetown Middle School, in court history. Hometown Piperato administered the Oath of Allegiance to 79 new citizens. The ceremony was for new citizens from 53 different countries.

	53 countries represented:
Afghanistan	1
Australia	2
Canada	7
China	1
Colombia	2
Costa Rica	1
Cuba	2
Ecuador	1
El Salvador	3
Guatemala	2
Haiti	1
Hungary	1
India	2
Indonesia	1
Ireland	1
Jamaica	3
Jamaica	2

Jaffe and Kenneth Zebrowski Jr. and County Legislators Ed Day and Harriet Cornell. *Rockland County Times* publisher Armand Miele and managing editor Dylan Skriloff also spoke at the event, blasting the MTA on behalf of the newspaper's readers. Approximately 50 people attended the meeting held at the Holiday Inn

---

Above, Right and Below Right:
Rockland County Times reports on the people raising their voices.

• • • • •

Below: A personal message from an American hero.

Healthcare Protest in New City

Armand, with my deepest personal regards,

Ronald Reagan

"Rally in the Rain"

If the Majority Doesn't Rule, Who Does?

In junior high school, I learned the acronym "SPAR," to remember our nation's Bill of Rights. The teacher posed with his fists up and said, "Think of a boxer training to fight, so you can remember what our country is all about."

S is for freedom of speech;

P is for freedom of the press;

A is for freedom of assembly; and

R is for freedom of religion.

I wonder if they teach the same thing in schools today. I don't think so. Many of our schoolteachers today are still of the Jane Fonda and Bill Clinton generation. During the Vietnam War, Jane Fonda went behind enemy lines and took pictures with enemy soldiers, to show her support for communist Vietnam. She should have been arrested for aiding and abetting the enemy, but she got away with it. Bill Clinton, as a young man, participated in demonstrations against the United States where protesters burned our flag, yet became the nation's president. Celebrities and political leaders from this generation discourage us from learning respect and reverence for our American freedoms.

As long as we have the freedom to control our individual lives, we have everything. If government gets control of our lives by curtailing our individual rights, we have a problem. Go to Zimbabwe, and find out what it is to lose your freedom of speech and freedom of assembly. The government there is not only oppressive, it is corrupt and ineffective. As of 2003, inflation was more than 8000 percent; by 2009 it was so far off the charts that the Zimbabwe dollar became meaningless. Unemployment was more than 80 percent in 2003, and there was practically no food. Don't like Zimbabwe? Try Saudi Arabia, where teenagers can be sentenced to death, and any criminal defendant can be tortured. Maybe you'd like Iran better, where they still have public hangings, and a woman can be put to death for adultery. In China, the government forces abortions. The Chinese government also controls all the media. And don't look for any deals in a Chinese court, because 99 percent of all criminal trials end in a guilty verdict.

This brings me to socialism, a word we are afraid to discuss when it comes to American government, but a very simple concept. Socialists base their economic theory on redistribution of wealth. In order to redistribute the wealth, the government must, of course, have power over people's individual wealth—and that can mean earnings, real property, or anything an individual can own. When government has this much power, it is only a step away from having absolute power. With the wrong person in control, a socialist government has the power to take away individual rights and become a dictatorship.

Socialism takes power out of the hands of the people, and when the people lose power, their freedoms start to die.

In 2008, I made a prediction. I said that in 20 years, if the government went through with the $700 billion so-called "bailout" of Wall Street, the U.S. would become a socialist, if not a communist country. Following the bailout, Congress has ownership stakes in all the banks. Next they will set wages throughout the country, and then they will own the businesses too. Small businesses won't be able to compete. We see this happening in 2010, with high unemployment and the majority of workers being employed by the government, rather than the private sector.

The socialists say that a government takeover is the only way to protect the economy. Remember that if the government takes over the economy, it takes another step toward absolute control.

Young people, remember that many of your parents and grandparents raised you here, and not in their home countries, in order to escape oppression, ethnic cleansing, and war. Americans also died fighting for the freedoms that you might take for granted.

So remember, when you vote, beware of inviting government control through socialism. Vote for the right person. It's not the name of a party you need to be concerned about, Republican, Democrat, liberal, or conservative. What's important is keeping America free.

Liberal Absolutists

January 31, 2010

Liberal absolutists are little dictators disguised as educators, scholars, and government advisors, who produce nothing for the economy but lots of theories on why communist ideals should govern the United States.

Everyone is afraid to speak against these absolutists with their Ph.D.s, and no wonder. They hold positions of great power in government and politics, although they are in the minority of the population. Today we have liberal absolutists in high positions everywhere. They control students, judges, lawyers, and the government workers under them. They have the power to destroy laws that support the free practice of religion, the exercise of individual rights, and the open expression of patriotism.

True American liberals support democracy, and feel that the people should remain in control of the government, although they also want the government to help those who cannot, on their own, achieve the basic promises of the American dream: plenty of food, comfortable shelter and clothing, and a good, solid education. In a way, all Americans are truly liberal, when it comes to helping their fellow man; the parties mainly differ in their opinions on how to get things done. Our founding fathers were the liberals of their day, and when they wrote the Constitution, which is supposed to be the foundation of all our laws, they were concerned with guaranteeing our freedom from government oppression. Our freedoms became the foundation for the American dream.

Liberal absolutists believe government should control the people, instead of the other way around. True liberals, don't fall into the web of the absolutists, who are using you. Individual rights must come before so-called public-interest reforms. The absolutists label conservatives as "right-wing" or "fundamentalist", as if preserving the Bill of Rights is obsolete or old-fashioned, while their socialist programs are more modern and progressive. Absolutists may preach that if you're not a socialist you have no heart, but remember the saying: a socialist over the age of 30 has no head. The socialist and communist ideals spouted all the time by the liberal absolutists failed in places like the Soviet Union, bringing about corruption, poverty, and oppression, yet the Absolutists want us to believe that their way will be different.

I wonder if people who side with the absolutists can imagine what life would be like if communists or socialists were to come into power. In Russia, it took only 10,000 card-carrying Communists in charge to control millions of people.

The Soviet Union owned everything in its domain, even the clothes on the people's backs. The state redistributed land, houses, and businesses. They printed new money, so that people's savings became worthless. The house a family had built and owned for years was not theirs anymore, and it was divided among strangers. The card-carrying Communists lived in families' homes, and made the rules about who could share bedrooms, who was allowed in the kitchen, who cleaned the bathrooms. Children spied on their parents, families spied on each other.

Kangaroo courts created new laws. Forget about freedom of speech; those who spoke against communism publicly were murdered. No freedom of the press, either. The state printed all the newspapers, and were the only ones allowed to do so. Freedom of assembly? Those who spoke against communism were murdered, and those who assembled to listen to them were slaughtered without mercy. Freedom of religion wasn't even a question, because religion was not allowed at all.

I ask all of the liberal absolutist sympathizers to live the life of a communist or socialist, or as the citizen of a dictatorship, for a short time. Follow the old saying, to really know someone, walk in his shoes for a day.

To the true, innocent liberals: if the absolutists take over, will they give you a membership card? Will they guarantee you the Bill of Rights?

———

How Badly Do We Need Cheap Labor?

December 3, 2009

Would you barter your 10-year-old son for 46 pounds of wheat a month for six years, or your five-year-old for half of that amount? This was the going deal in Afghanistan in 2002. Parents bartered children in order to feed the rest of the family.

One restaurant owner said, "It is cheaper to buy boys than to hire boys." I hope he didn't mean that. When you hire a boy, he still has his parents to go home to for the necessities. All you have to do is treat him humanely during the workday. In the case of a bartered boy, on top of paying the family, the master would have to feed, clothe, and shelter the boy; he would see his parents only perhaps once in six months. I would hope that the restaurant owner would spend more per day on a bartered boy's care and his family's price than he would on a hired boy's daily wages.

All this was reported in the New York Times ("Children as Barter in a Famished Land," Barry Bearak, March 8, 2002), and I thought it was a worthy subject to write about in my column. Here in America we always cry out for human rights. I wonder whether we know what we are crying about. The suffering and hardship in Afghanistan cannot be handled overnight. Africa, China, and all developing countries face similar issues.

The way I see it, human rights abuses have been going on since the beginning of civilization. In America and the rest of the industrialized world, we have worked for centuries to develop real governments, to fight these kinds of abuses of power, but when we lower the bar for immigration, we are bringing ourselves back to the level of developing countries. Industrialized countries have been accepting increasing numbers of immigrants from third world countries, drastically changing to accommodate these new immigrants.

When we open our borders to any and everyone, we open our culture to the influence of people who are accustomed to bartering their children. Are we really interested in human rights, or are we, too, bartering for cheap labor? Are we bringing in a new sickness, accommodating the dishonesty not only of those who cross the border illegally, but those who welcome them with low-paying jobs?

The only way we should help immigrants is the way we did with the first waves of European immigrants that came here looking for work at the turn of the century. Immigrants had to have a physical examination, present records of who they were, and what their reasons were for entering our country. Most of all, they had to have a sponsor who would take responsibility for them, either a member of their family or the government. As a result, so many responsible, bright people were admitted to this country after World War II and the Korean War that the phenomenon was called the "brain drain." Professional and educated people, not only from Europe, but from Asia and all over the world, fled from their war-torn homelands to pursue the American dream.

Immigration laws that require honor and honesty from those seeking to come to the U.S. will help us to get our country back on solid footing, for the sake of Americans and Americans-to-be.

———

Preferred Minorities

December 17, 2009

I'm of Italian descent. I'm a minority, and so is anyone whose ancestors immigrated to this country in the last century. This country is made up of minorities of all colors, nationalities, and religions. We all know this. It's been said many times and in many different ways that our diversity makes America the strongest nation in the world.

Today there are "preferred minorities": immigrants with Spanish surnames; people of African heritage from all over the world, whose background has nothing to do with American slavery; people of certain races and traditions, be it American Indian or Hasidic Jewish; women of every color and nationality;

and so on. I say they are preferred minorities because they are the ones permitted to take advantage of affirmative action laws, which were created not for immigrants or minorities per se, but for the sake of blacks in this country who were held back for generations because of discrimination.

The first affirmative action laws were justifiable and good. Being of Italian descent, I know about hatred, jealousy, and discrimination. There was a time that a family with an Italian name couldn't get an apartment in many places, including the Grand Concourse in the Bronx. I will never forget a woman who said, "The Guineas are coming into the neighborhood." Racists are still out there. Only five years ago an ex-policeman called me a "Guinea bastard."

The worst scenario against Italians took place on March 14, 1891 in New Orleans. Eleven Italian-Americans were charged with killing the chief of police. There was a long trial, and all were found not guilty. After the verdict was announced, the men were dragged out of jail and lynched: a local group shot and then hanged all eleven men.

I mention this story to show that before affirmative action laws, the only difference between black Americans and Americans of foreign descent was the color of our skin. When affirmative action came into being, we Italian-Americans and other American immigrants needed it as much as the American black people did. Italian names such as Lee Iacocca and Antonin Scalia were, at one time, taboo in the mainstream world.

One advantage the Italians had was that as people with lighter skin, we could just change our names in order to get jobs: Pesce became Fish, Cucina became Cook, Bianco became White, etc. (if nothing else, I taught you some Italian words). We sneaked in where black Americans couldn't. I remember being embarrassed to be a white person while traveling by train from New York to Florida. You boarded in New York and sat wherever there was a seat, until you got to Washington, DC. Here, whites and blacks were separated—different seats and toilet facilities—both on the trains and in the stations. Black people weren't permitted in many restaurants, even though most of the workers were black.

As un-American as segregation was, I feel the preferred minority practices in place today are just as discriminatory. It's become reverse discrimination. Discrimination in any form is unjust, and injustice should have no place in America. The federal and state governments finally woke up, and made laws against hatred, but I believe that these preferred minorities are taking advantage of a good thing. This is one of the things destroying America.

I was running for a political office several years ago, and was invited to speak to high school students of all different nationalities and colors. There were many good questions. And then a question came from a black student about how I stood on affirmative action. I looked this student in the eye and I said what I've written here: affirmative action was appropriate when it started, but it has now passed its time. Then I said, "I see affirmative action ruining students like yourself, for the simple reason that you become lax. Your thought becomes, 'Why should I work as hard as a white student? I go ahead of him whether I study or not.'"

I believed that then, and I believe that now. Even an ultra-liberal person must see there is something wrong when the child of a doctor with preferred minority status doesn't have to pay a college application fee, and it costs a white miner's child $150. Preferred minority status has to go. It does not serve the hard worker, it makes people lax, and it has become reverse discrimination.

———

Unions In Government Means We're Governed By Unions

May 20, 2010

On New Year's Day of 1966, John Lindsay, on his first day as mayor of New York City, was confronted by Mike Quill, the founder of the Transit Workers' Union (TWU). The TWU's contract with the city was set to expire that same day, and Quill demanded a wage increase. Lindsay refused. The TWU called a strike and shut down the city, completely halting subway and bus service for twelve days. The traffic was almost impassable. New York was in such a mess that Governor Rockefeller offered to call in the National Guard. Lindsay, the jerk, said no.

After this, it officially became illegal for public workers to strike in New York State, but the parade started anyway. In 1968, the teachers' union went on strike for four months, and there was also a Broadway strike for three days. Let's not forget the sanitation strike for nine days. One of the firefighters' big strikes was in 1970, when over 8000 firefighters and other workers belonging to AFSCME District Council 37 walked off their jobs for two days. Strikers included personnel on the city's drawbridges and sewer plants. Drawbridges over the Harlem River were locked in the "up" position, barring transit by automobiles. Even the police engaged in a slowdown, and the firefighters threatened job actions. New York became even more of a mess.

Politicians are more interested in getting elected than in helping the people. Instead of putting the striking city workers in jail, Lindsay let them destroy New York. Only President Ronald Reagan had the guts, when the air traffic controllers went on strike in 1981, to fire them. Why isn't the same done to any government union strikers?

The only reason is that the unions donate to any politician that votes in their favor. This must stop. There should be a law against politicians taking money from unions. Not too many years ago, Congress passed a law to prevent the unions from forcing members to donate to union-supported politicians, but in New York and other states, the unions are permitted to contribute plenty to local candidates.

Unions are never satisfied. They can put any company, even the government, out of business, and will eventually destroy our country and themselves. The government and union workers today are sharing in the profits of the economy.

The only difference now, between a union and a government body, is that union leaders don't have to run for election.

Union officials have become legal racketeers, and they have a lot of politicians on their side. Their only concern is to get theirs, and to heck with everyone else. The teachers' union continues to threaten, and the hospitals now do the same thing. Whatever happened to public service? It's the taxpayers that are the servants today. When these unions go on strike, without care for the people they serve, they should all be fired. They can be replaced.

The union workers have become an illegal monopoly, causing rising prices and destroying the work ethic. Workers in the private sector, without job guarantees, so often take second or third jobs to keep afloat. Mom-and-pop businesses are suffering, putting in long hours to barely support their families. The small business owner keeps his own books, pays for his own health insurance, and rarely takes vacations. All these hardworking people in the private sector are rewarded only by paying higher taxes to the government, who pay themselves first, then take care of the unions. Outrageous union salaries reward those who produce nothing for the economy but problems.

Government and union-controlled industries are the biggest competitors for private-sector and small-business workers today. We have more union and government workers than are needed on the job. When a new government administration comes in, it always adds on more jobs for its supporters. With union jobs, the union members are feather-bedding, and they know it. Some do nothing, telling anyone who complains, "It's not my job." The government backs this up by insisting, at times, that only union workers can do certain jobs. Big corporations have to employ card-carrying union workers, and private-sector workers are not allowed to work in a union shop.

I repeat, wherever the unions have power, they have a monopoly. What happened to the law?

———

Outsourcing Saved Union Fees and Ruined the United States

February 11, 2010

The blame for the outsourcing problem we have today falls square on the crooked union heads. These union heads are slowly destroying the American economy, because they are not business people. They just see things one way: big corporations make all the money, and unions are entitled to a cut. The demands never end. They are never concerned with whether a business is making a profit or loss.

To make a profit and stay in business, any company's wages will always lag behind prices. It's a simple weighing of expenses against profits. High wages create high prices, which will kill a business. Prices must dictate wages, not the other way around.

Because of the union demands for increasing wages, many American corporations were forced to move their operations overseas to stay in business. They couldn't afford to pay union wages. The government allowed this exporting of jobs, because they knew the unions were putting the squeeze on businesses, and outsourcing allowed the businesses to keep from going under. Even President Clinton did not do anything to stop outsourcing, despite the unions' support of his administration. That's how outsourcing became a regular part of the American economy.

As another example of how union interference changed a big part of the economy, look at New York's port. New York has the largest natural port in the world. Because of this, New York's harbor was the busiest port in the world for years. Any business having to do with the ports became a bonanza for the crooks that formed unions and took command of New York City's terminals. The same thing happened in California and other big ports. The unions' crazy demands made it very expensive for the owners to run the piers, preventing them from upgrading and improving their businesses with new containers and modern computerized equipment, and so they closed down in New York and California. All the shipping business to the United States eventually went to huge new terminals in New Jersey, Baltimore, New Orleans and the Carolinas, where the new container ships did not need the natural ports.

We are witnessing something similar with our cars. Chrysler, Ford, and General Motors are good examples. To keep union wages high in Detroit, the government outsourced the assembly of cars to Mexico and other parts of the world, where labor is cheaper. Doing this allowed the companies to save enough money to subsidize the union.

In Mexico, they pay automobile workers $150 a week. In Detroit, the union automobile workers doing the same work earn, on average, more than $1,500 a week. At one time, General Motors was paying 10,000 laid-off workers after their plant closed, because, due to union rules, they could not be transferred to another plant more than 50 miles from their original place of work. Even when not working, employees were still entitled to pay. Figure it out. If it weren't for outsourcing, it would cost 10 times more to build a car—and what would that do to the sticker price? This all happened because the government gives in to unions at almost any cost. Political leaders who are this far under the unions' influence should be voted out of office.

No matter how we look at it, the government going back to Clinton's administration put outsourcing into place to save the country from another Great Depression. I just read that an American computer company is spending $30 million for a factory in South Vietnam to make computer chips. If not for the unions, that factory could have been in the U.S. Yet the unions are fighting like mad to put companies like Wal-Mart out of business because of outsourcing. Just consider: what would happen to our economy if outsourcing was outlawed? If the unions want to join in saving the American economy and themselves, they have to learn that business survives by keeping prices reasonable. High wages create high prices, which will kill a business. Prices must dictate wages, not the other way around.

The worst thing that happened was when unions were allowed to organize government workers. Municipal union workers can put any local government in bankruptcy. The proof is the situation today, where all of the state governments are in trouble. In government, the "price tag" is on the services that we pay taxes for, and the government thinks it can just raise taxes whenever the unions demand a higher wage. Government wages have nothing to do with the government making a profit or loss. The government just signs the paycheck, and has us jerks, the taxpayers, foot the bill.

———

Troublemaking Activists, Get the Facts Straight on Indian Point!

April 21, 2011

The two Governors Cuomo have been enemies of Indian Point for years, and now Andrew Cuomo is in the position to either please the alarmists, or to wake up and face reality. Licenses for the plant's reactors are set to expire in 2013 and 2015. But where are the new sources of power to replace what's generated by Indian Point? The plant has been here for 50 years, servicing us with no complaints about price. The politicians never take that into account. They only play follow the leader to gather votes.

Most of us depend on Indian Point for our energy. The politicians and the activists don't think about who will pay the higher energy bills if the plant is shut down.

Many of the activists that want to shut the plant down don't even live here. One group tried without success to prove their case in court: their claim, that the plant hurt the fish in the river, was shot down. They used these numbers: 2.4 billion gallons of water, over a billion fish per year. Can you imagine billions of fish in that one small part of the Hudson River to begin with, let alone that over a billion were killed every year for 50 years by one power plant? Where in hell do they get their figures? The activists also forced the plant to spend a fortune on new alarm systems and higher security, in case of terrorist attack.

Activists continue to campaign for the shutdown of Indian Point, because of the thousands-to-one possibility that an earthquake like the one in Japan could hit New York, and the even slimmer chance that a tsunami could travel all that way up the Hudson River from New York harbor. In that case, New York would be so completely destroyed that Indian Point would be the least of any survivors' worries. And in the meantime, Cuomo has no plan for how to replace the energy. If we get rid of Indian Point, New Yorkers throughout New York City and the Hudson Valley will need a new source of power. Will Cuomo and his phonies pay the new, higher prices for us? They have already chased Mirant, a company that paid $50 million a year in school and real estate taxes, out of Rockland.

Look at how the activist troublemakers hurt Queens County, where people pay the highest utility bills in the country, and where Con Edison is criticized repeatedly for service failures. It isn't Con Edison's fault. The wacky environmentalists, activists, and the politicians who go along with them are at fault.

It was the first Governor Cuomo, Mario, who listened to the environmentalists and prevented Queens from getting affordable power. Construction on the Shoreham Power Plant, the twin of the Millstone 1 plant in Connecticut, was to begin in 1971. Both plants were ordered in the mid-60's; Millstone 1 was completed by 1970 at a cost of $101 million. After years of protests by activists, the Shoreham plant was finally built by 1986 at a cost of $5.5 billion. Can you imagine, once the plant was ready to operate, Cuomo took the side not of the people, for their health and welfare, but of the demonstrators! He denied approving the plant, and put pressure on the New York public utility companies to go along with him.

Cuomo got his way, and the families in Queens are suffering for it today. He made a deal with LILCO, the Queens electric company who couldn't afford the $500,000 to close and dismantle the plant. The deal cost the State one dollar, and LILCO gained billions of dollars in utility rates increases. I wonder where those demonstrators are today. Sweating it out and paying huge utility bills? Probably not. I'm willing to bet that the complainers are all gone. It's the ones who stayed, and also the new people coming in, not knowing about the huge utility bills, who suffer.

I am writing this to remind Rocklanders that the activists who are against Indian Point could put us in the same position as the people in Queens. We have over 100 nuclear plants around the country. Indian Point has been here for 50 years, so get off of their backs. Remember, the activists and the politicians don't think about all the pros and cons, and they don't think about the cost to taxpayers. They only want the prestige of getting in the papers and getting elected. They play follow-the-leader, without thinking about the repercussions.

Governor Mario Cuomo was voted out of office, and I hope that New Yorkers will remember that they are still suffering for what he did. Our state legislators had better wake up, stop horsing around, and get going on the need for affordable energy.

———

President Ronald Reagan and the Making of Real History

April 2, 2009

I remember when Ronald Reagan was the governor of California. He had won an election against Governor Brown, who left California a deficit of $5 billion. After eight years in office, Ronald Reagan left a surplus of $5 billion for the next governor. He became president of the United States in 1980.

I want to tell the history of what I have lived through, and give credit where it is due. Much is owed to President Ronald W. Reagan.

Reagan lifted a veil of malaise that went back to President Franklin Roosevelt. Roosevelt was known to have socialist views, and was a communist sympathizer. He helped communist Russia in many ways, before and during World War II. There were even federally funded programs here in New York that collected clothes and donations for communist Russia.

During World War II, FDR gave in to Russia at the Yalta Conference. He did not protest when Stalin demanded one third of the territory of Poland, and referred to Stalin as "Uncle Joe" and "a good friend." Poland had been an American ally during World War I, but due to FDR's double-crossing, communist Stalin eventually took over all of Poland.

The Great Double-Crosser also should have known the Japanese were on their way to bomb Pearl Harbor. His secretary of state warned him to expect an attack from Japan at any time, but Roosevelt didn't notify the American military. In fact, his administration's official position was to let Japan commit the first hostile act. This should never have been a surprise attack. The tragedy at Pearl Harbor was a gutless personal fault of Franklin Roosevelt.

Franklin Roosevelt's socialist ideas kept us in the Great Depression for eight years. Communism was rampant, and became strong during his administration. Communists had parades in New York City. If it weren't for states' rights under the Constitution, we could easily have had national communism under FDR. People want to list him as a great president? He almost destroyed American freedom.

Next came President Harry Truman. After World War II, Truman couldn't get the country going, so he devised the "52-20" club. An out-of-work military person would get $20 a week for 52 weeks from the federal government. Truman feared going back into a depression, so created the Korean War in an effort to pump the country up. Thousands of soldiers died in what

Truman called a "police action," and afterwards, it was called "the forgotten war."

Let the Korean veterans tell you their stories, and ask them, was Truman a great president? Like hell he was. I was drafted during the Korean War. In the Army hospital, I witnessed soldiers whose hands and feet were frostbitten. Truman was in such a hurry to send these guys over that they didn't have winter uniforms. In the newsreels, the soldiers had to wrap newspapers around their legs to keep warm. Their guns froze and couldn't fire. Many soldiers suffered and died, not from bullet wounds, but because they weren't equipped correctly. Anyone who calls Truman great has been reading the wrong history book.

Next, President Kennedy had 15,000 Marines standing by to aid Vietnam President Diem in case of a communist invasion. Kennedy said he would give full support to non-communist President Diem, but failed to act when communists attacked, killed Diem, and overthrew his administration.

Kennedy lied to the Cubans too, refusing to keep America's promise to support the Cuban freedom fighters as they fought an impossible battle at the Bay of Pigs. After the communists took over, the Cuban world wept and wondered what had happened to America.

Next we had President Johnson and the Vietnam War. Johnson kept increasing the armed forces, despite the obvious ineffectiveness of our military efforts. He was a disaster. Before his next term he resigned, and would not seek the presidency again.

President Nixon and Vice President Agnew were doing great until Agnew had to leave. He pleaded no contest to allegations of tax evasion during his time as governor of Maryland. Gerald Ford became vice president. Watergate ended Nixon's career, and Ford was appointed to finish Nixon's term.

James Carter, an unknown, became president after Ford. This was the beginning of the end of America. Inflation rose to 12 percent, and interest rates, to 18 percent. Iran took over the American Embassy, and held 52 Americans hostage for more than a year. The country lost all credibility. Out of shame, no one put the American flag out on holidays. I was in Paris, France, during this time, and many money exchange agencies wouldn't take a hundred-dollar bill, fearing the value of the dollar would plummet. The world looked at America as a defeated country.

President Reagan faced all these problems, and he succeeded in turning things around. He brought America back stronger than ever by proving he was an American first, not a party member. He reduced income taxes from 70 percent to 28 percent. Inflation dropped, interest rates dropped. The hostages that were held in Iran for over a year were released.

Reagan's greatest accomplishment was his assistance in the defeat of communism in the Soviet Union, without one bullet being fired. He called for Soviet Premier Mikael Gorbachev to allow greater economic and personal freedoms, and met with Gorbachev many times, in support of new Soviet policies that eventually lead to the dissolution of the Soviet Union. Although it is rarely mentioned, the right to practice religion was restored in the communist countries.

One day, maybe people will remember Reagan's presidency for what it was: one of the proudest eras in America's history. The lies of Soviet communism were finally exposed, and American freedoms regained their old glory. Today's Americans should never forget our most precious ideals of life, liberty, and the pursuit of happiness.

Seated: Frankie and Mary, me and Boots, Jimmy and Josie, Catherine.
Standing: A friend, Augie and Susie, and Bill, Catherine's husband.
Circa 1972

Seated: John, me, Boots, Lulu.
Standing: Lionel, Donna Lee, Paul, Armand, Michael, and Ken

Conclusion

First of all, I want to thank everyone who helped to get "Born Minus" published and into readers' hands: my daughter, Donna Lee Miele; my editors, Sylke Jackson and Bill Herman; my son-in-law, Ken Herndon; and the staff at the Rockland County Times.

During the writing of this book my health has been up and down, and in 2010 declined to where I did not believe I would see this book finished. In June, 2010 I received a new kidney and a new life at the University of Pittsburg Medical Center. I want to thank all the people who have been involved with my care. I especially honor the memory of my kidney donor, who I will never know, but to whom I will be always grateful.

Of course, I have a few closing words for my family, but the rest of you readers might get something out of it, too.

When I was still in my 30s, a friend said to me, "Don't you wish you could go back to being a boy again? No worries, no problems."

I think that after reading this book, you might know what my answer was: "No way."

I've said it a few times in this book, and I'll say it again: you learn from the past, but you must live for the future. If anything, I would go back to see my mother and father again, and my Delia. Other than that, I wouldn't re-live another moment. I wouldn't go back and fight through another battle.

Thinking back, I wonder if those who are nostalgic for the old days simply feel uneasy about all the changes that have gone on in America since I was a boy. When I stop and think about it, I wonder whether it was all for the good? Corporate America places more value on employees who possess degrees but no good sense; so-called educated Americans consider themselves above manual labor; and when their lifestyles won't support them hiring maids and landscapers at good wages, they bring immigrants in through the back door to keep themselves looking wealthy. I wonder what will happen to today's American lifestyle, when the immigrants smarten up and get their degrees? Without immigrants to fill the gap, maybe Americans will be back to the same lifestyle my parents had.

I hope that I've been able to give readers some idea of what should be important to the American lifestyle, no matter whether we face war or poverty, or whether we must struggle with poor political leadership. First and foremost is family.

It's a pity, but people love to hear parents say bad things about their children. They think it's funny. That's not me. I say, if you can't say anything good about your own child, there is a problem, and the problem starts with the parent.

To Donna Lee, I would hope to hear from you that I was everything a parent should be: loving, caring, honest, everything super and good. Of course, like many parents, I know I have been over-protective too. I never want to see you, your husband, or my grandchildren taken advantage of. I found out the hard way that many so-called friends were only concerned with themselves. I trusted and believed in people, only to have them double-cross me.

Still, I would say that you must trust in people, and help when you can. Don't lose your true friends, the people with whom you share understanding, with whom you can be honest, and whose company you most enjoy.

Look out for jealousy in yourself. Once it creeps in, it will affect all your habits and your relationships, and prevent you from enjoying your life.

I feel that I have given you the best tools I know of. I feel gratified to have you and Ken, and know you will carry on with your family to the utmost.

To my grandchildren especially, who are the youngest members of this new generation of Americans, living a lifestyle of instant gratification, I say, be careful! Watch out for that feeling that you never have enough. When you are feeling lonely or like something is missing, come out of your shell.

There is always someone out there who is concerned for you. Give that person a chance. Find a hobby, fall in love, get out into the fresh air, see what life is all about, and wonder. Look up to the sky and try to reach the clouds that are roaming, the sun and the evening stars. Walk on the seaside with your shoes off. Now do you know how fortunate you are?

Armand Miele
July 8, 2011

CPSIA information can be obtained at www.ICGtesting.com
Printed in the USA
270252BV00002B/4/P